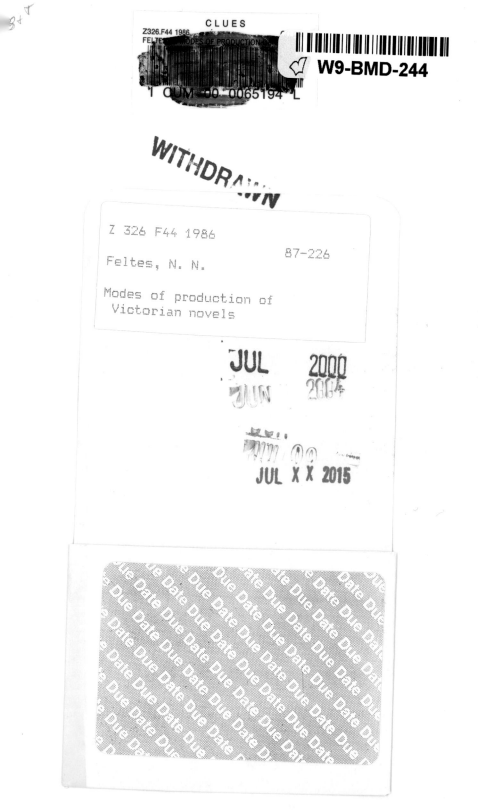

Modes of
Production of
VICTORIAN
NOVELS

Modes of
Production of
VICTORIAN
NOVELS

N.N. Feltes

The University of Chicago Press
Chicago and London

N. N. Feltes is professor of English at York University
in Ontario, Canada.

The University of Chicago Press, Chicago 60637
The University of Chicago Press, Ltd., London
© 1986 by The University of Chicago
All rights reserved. Published 1986
Printed in the United States of America

95 94 93 92 91 90 89 88 87 86   5 4 3 2 1

Library of Congress Cataloging-in-Publication Data

Feltes, N. N. (Norman N.)
    Modes of production of Victorian novels.

    Includes index.
    1. Fiction—Publishing—Great Britain—History—19th
century.   2. Publishers and publishing—Great Britain—
History—19th century.   3. English fiction—19th century
—History and criticism.   4. Authors and publishers—
Great Britain—History—19th century.   5. Authors and
readers—Great Britain—History—19th century.
6. Serial publication of books.   7. Publishers and
publishing—Economic aspects—Great Britain.   8. Fiction
—Authorship—Economic aspects.   I. Title.
Z326.F44   1986   070.5′0941   86-6927
ISBN 0-226-24117-3

to Liz

Contents

Preface

This book presents studies of the production of five English novels, published at roughly twenty-year intervals from 1836 to 1910; that spacing was a consideration in my choosing to focus on *Pickwick Papers, Henry Esmond, Middlemarch, Tess of the D'Urbervilles* and *Howards End,* to try to understand historically the material conditions for the production of Victorian novels generally. I have regretted that the numerous empirical studies of different features of Victorian novel production should be bracketed as "specialist," or "background," as they have been by the dominant critical modes. Indeed, when a colleague, years ago, used to ask candidates at professional interviews which literary critical book of the last twenty years or so they would like to have written, I would consider to myself Kathleen Tillotson's *Novels of the Eighteen-Forties.* The colleague would often then ask which book the candidate would like to rewrite, and I have since then come to think that I would myself now want to give the same answer: Tillotson's *Novels of the Eighteen-Forties.* Not to presume literally to rewrite that fine work, but rather finally to *use* it, and to use the work of John Carter and Graham Pollard, Richard Altick and Royal Gettmann, and others, more intensively than those historical and bibliographical materials have been used up to now. Thus another consideration in planning this book has been diversity of format of first publication: these five novels represent monthly part-publication, three-volume-, magazine serial-, bi-monthly part-, and single-volume-publication. My purpose has been to demonstrate through these differences of format and the other publishing details catalogued in the empirical studies a historical view which disrupts the text/ background distinction, insisting that these historical circumstances not be relegated to a slightly subordinate level of special interest. This book argues the importance of such details as format as being the concrete mediations of the historical in the production of novels, determining in complex ways the actual production of a particular novel and tracing themselves in its text and its own production of ideology.

The line of approach is, thus, marxist, assuming a materialist historical analysis, taking the point of view of production, using the concept of modes of production. The period of history which these chapters cover, from 1836 (and before) to 1910 (and after), is the period of the transformation in England from a precapitalist, petty commodity mode to a fully capitalist literary mode of production, and my analysis of the forms of this transformation strives to be as theoretically precise as it is historically specific, drawing on the tradition of marxist analysis of the transition to the capitalist mode of production, as it draws on the empirical studies to situate that analysis in the sphere of literary production. This book draws especially on the theoretical work of Louis Althusser, Nicos Poulantzas, and Terry Eagleton: for example, the book conceives of Victorian England in Poulantzas's terms, as a social formation, a complex unity dominated by a certain mode of production, itself determined, "in the last instance," by the economic;[1] or again, referring to that social formation, "ideology" would signify "certain of Victorian England's ways of signifying itself";[2] and again, the ideology produced by each of the literary texts "interpellates," or invokes its willing reader as a (free) subject.[3] The book argues the analytic value of this problematic in addressing the history of Victorian novel production.

My only theoretical contribution to this framework of

analysis has been to locate the commodity-form in the different literary modes of production. The objectivity of commodities as values, Marx comments, is especially difficult to grasp: as Falstaff said of Dame Quickly, one knows not where to have it.[4] I have organized my own grasp of literary commodities by distinguishing the commodity-form of petty-commodity production, the "commodity-*book*," from that of a capitalist literary mode of production, the "commodity-*text*." The first two chapters, on *Pickwick Papers* and *Henry Esmond*, discuss those terms and use them to locate each novel within the larger historical transition. In each of the remaining chapters I suggest that the transition itself is traced most broadly in the efforts of publishers and authors effectively to produce a commodity-text, whose surplus value each party struggles to claim. Those struggles, too, are historically determined in complex ways; gender determinations, for example, might in each case be analyzed, with greater or lesser difficulty, as I have analyzed gender determinations specific to the production of *Middlemarch*.

My effort towards historical specificity is meant also to avoid any implied teleology: as capitalist social relations permeate the Victorian social formation, shaping social phenomena as commodities, so literary texts are distinguished and transformed, along with the forces and relations of their production—the order here implying no particular sequence, but rather relative autonomy and overdetermination. This book is not meant as a narrative account of the transition towards capitalist novel production. Rather it assumes, and derives, that transition in a historical analysis of particular novels. And just as I do not argue that the economic forms "gave way," the one to the next, or that one set of social or political relations "led to" or "laid the groundwork for" a further "stage" in the development of book production, so I do not suggest, on the level of the text, a sort of economic determinist "great tradition." The canonicity of the novels is irrelevant to my study of their production; my concern has been with technological and ideological changes, the constitution and reconstitution of power relations in publishing, the constitution and recon-

stitution of "audiences." And, while providing no "readings" or interpretations, I have followed out the ways in
which these determinate historical processes are traced in
the text, how each text, in Eagleton's phrase, encodes within
itself "how, by whom and for whom it was produced."[5] I
have not provided readings of the novels precisely because I
am trying to discuss each work from the point of view of its
production and not, as in other critical practices, as object of
consumption, "modifying the work in order to assimilate it
more thoroughly."[6] The themes and devices I do examine I
am interested in for their determinate place in the process
of production, whatever might be said elsewhere of their
contribution to a unified totality, or to its meaning. As I
point out in the chapter in which I most persist in discussing
themes, Chapter 2, I mean to address those formal elements
not as constituents of a "unity" or "essence" of the text of
Henry Esmond but rather as traces of its particular literary
mode of production.

I have incurred a great number of personal obligations in
the course of producing this book, and I am glad to be able
to acknowledge them. I am very grateful to the Faculty of
Arts, York University, for a year's Leave Fellowship which
allowed me to complete the manuscript, and to the staff of
York's Secretarial Services who so patiently and skillfully
processed it. I am grateful as well to the staffs of the Robarts
Library, University of Toronto, the Scott Library, York
University, the Bodleian Library, Oxford, and the New-
berry Library, Chicago. The editors of *Literature and History*
have kindly allowed me to include, as Chapter 1 of this book,
a revised version of a paper which originally appeared in
that journal. I have a long-standing debt of gratitude to
Jerome Beaty for his continuing advice and friendship, and
to Terry Eagleton for his friendship, also, and for his
teaching. I am very thankful to Heather Murray who read a
version of the whole manuscript and advised me on it,
and to Scott Bennett, Penny Boumelha, Linda Hutcheon,
Richard Landon, George Levine, Michael Lund, Pamela
McCallum, Peter Morgan, Daphne Read, Dorothy Smith,
and Ann Wilson, all of whom read parts of the manuscript

at various times and counseled me. I value their help very much and know how much I have benefited from it. I remain, of course, wholly responsible for the errors and faults which persist.

One

The Production of a Commodity-Text: The Moment of *Pickwick*

"More than *Childe Harold* or *Waverley*, more than *Adam Bede* or *The Heir of Redclyffe* . . . , *Pickwick* was the most sensational triumph in nineteenth-century publishing." George Ford's discussion of the reviews, Richard Altick's study of circulation figures, John Butt and Kathleen Tillotson's account of Dickens at work transforming the shilling part-issue, all point to the uniqueness of Dicken's first triumph.[1] All of these are "pioneer" explorations of various empirical facts surrounding the appearance of *Pickwick Papers* and so, focused on those sorts of specific information, none can attempt an explanation of the event. A literary historian would need to read these accounts, the stories of the publication of *Pickwick*, symptomatically, or dialectically,[2] to explain the historical event and its significance. The general outline of the story of the publication of *Pickwick Papers* is well known: in early 1836 the new firm of Chapman and Hall planned with the popular illustrator Robert Seymour for a series of sporting prints in shilling numbers, and they invited the young journalist, Charles Dickens, whose recent collected *Sketches By Boz* had had a moderate success, to write the accompanying text. Dickens joined the enterprise as an ambitious, opinionated junior partner, differing from the start with Seymour about the precedence of illustration over text, and over the proposed rural setting and the "sporting" interests of the Pickwickians. Seymour, who was harried by personal worries, committed suicide just as the second number was being published; new illustrators were sought and Hablot K. Brown (Phiz) hired, and Dickens was left the dominant partner. His ideas for the Pickwickians quickly prevailed; in the fourth number he introduced into the story Sam Weller, who was especially applauded in the *Literary Gazette,* which reprinted Sam's monologues, and before the year was out Dickens was the most widely read author in England, with the instalments of *Pickwick* selling 40,000 copies each month, a success "unprecedented in the history of literature."[3]

That is a version of the standard account of the circumstances surrounding the publication of *Pickwick Papers.* Literary historians may differ over specific details and their significance—the relation of Seymour's depression to his differences with Dickens, the precise level of *Pickwick*'s initial success or the influence on that success of the intervention of Jerdan, the editor of the *Literary Gazette*[4]—but the implications of their conclusions are generally in agreement: the publication of *Pickwick Papers* marks the explosion of Dickens's "genius" upon the literary world. A series of accidents permitted that genius to flower and its comic essence to be discerned and encouraged early, so that *Pickwick Papers* might reach its inevitable and waiting audience. "Dickens and his publishers," writes Patten, "discovered the potential of serial publication virtually by accident," and Ford suggests that the appearance of *Pickwick* coincided with a "shift of taste."[5] Only occasionally does one find literary historians glancing towards historical explanations for the accidents or for Dickens's "genius." Patten, for example, speaking of part-issue, remarks that

> what forces made that format suddenly possible, and how the changes in publishing converged in 1836 and were connected by two shrewd, courageous, and lucky booksellers with the one man who could write letterpress for *all* the people, needs to be understood more fully than it has been so far.[6]

And Steven Marcus draws an "only partly fanciful" analogy between the language of *Pickwick* and "the take-off into self-sustained growth" of the Victorian economy, noting that a critic might work out elsewhere "the mediations that would provide it with substance."[7] What I am proposing is not at all fanciful, indeed risking perhaps more "banging the field-piece" than "twanging the lyre."[8] I would ignore genius, luck, and the shrewdness of Chapman and Hall; instead, I want to look at those historical processes which shaped and determined the material production of *Pickwick Papers*. For the publication of *Pickwick* took place within a determinate subensemble of emerging industrial capitalism, the production of written texts. Indeed *Pickwick Papers* marks the transition (the "explosion" or "take-off") from the petty-commodity production of books to the capitalist production of texts, and these are the changes which need to be understood more fully. We also need to understand the ways in which the literary text, *Pickwick Papers*, "bears the impress of its historical mode of production," how it "encodes within itself its own ideology of how, by whom and for whom it was produced";[9] this understanding also, finally, is part of my project.

We need not spend long on the transformation in the general mode of production which took place in Britain from 1750 to 1850, from simple or petty-commodity production[10] to industrial capitalism; I want merely to note some general forms of that transformation. As Hindess and Hirst point out: "It is not wage-labour and commodity production as such which define capitalism but the production and extraction of surplus-value as the dominant mode of appropriation of surplus-labor."[11] What defines precisely the capitalist mode of production is not a *specific form of ownership* of the means of production (that began around the sixteenth century) but a *specific form of control* over the labor process so as to produce surplus value.[12] These changes in the forces and relations of production slowly produced a very different market; as E. J. Hobsbawm describes the market of petty-commodity production:

> the available and prospective market—and it is the market which determines what a businessman produces—consists of the rich, who require luxury goods in small quantities, but with a high

profit-margin per sale, and the poor, who—if they are in the market economy at all, and do not produce their own consumer goods domestically or locally—have little money, are unaccustomed to novelties and suspicious of them, unwilling to consume standardized products and may not even be concentrated in cities or accessible to national manufacturers.

Industrial capitalism changed the market by "enabling production—within certain limits—to expand its own markets, if not actually to create them,"[13] and this was achieved through its characteristic control over the labor process. The usual accounts of publishing in the early nineteenth century, reluctant to speak of "modes of production," present rather a formless picture of publishing practice. Louis James alludes vaguely to "the feverish publishing activity that took place in the 1830s, and to a lesser extent in the previous decade," while another writer describes the discovery of "wove" paper, of new paper-making materials, and the invention of a paper-making machine and of the iron printing press as simply a "graphic confluence" around 1800.[14] But the transformation of the general mode of production necessarily determined the forces and relations in the subordinate sector of book production in particular ways, and it is these mediations, these changes in the social relations of production in a particular place at a particular time[15] that I want primarily to address, reinterpreting "the rise of the publisher," the rise of the "professional author," and the status of the "literary text."

For the formula, "the rise of the publisher," obscures the complexity of the historical changes in book production at the beginning of the nineteenth century. So does the word "bibliomania" which, while clearly gesturing towards the material effects of general economic change (speculation, etc.), is conventionally used simply to describe the frantic activity in the rare-book trade during the Napoleonic Wars which allowed booksellers to "rise" as "publishers": "Fortunes could be and were made in the antiquarian book trade, allowing many men [to] amass the capital to set up as publishers, where there were still greater profits to be

4

made."[16] The early years of the nineteenth century marked a significant change in the function and spirit of publishing, a "turn towards specialization," as booksellers and publishers became less and less "involved in each other's spheres."[17] These changes produced "a firm which wholesales its own books but does not wholesale anybody else's—the firm which organizes the production of a book, and then sells it direct to retailers all over the British Isles." Such a firm organized its market in the country by means of the literary reviews, commercial travelers, prospectuses and catalogues,[18] and these were, of course, dependent on the development of paved roads, fast coaches, canals, and eventually, railways. From the 1760s, provincial banks had begun to appear and London publishers could replace cumbersome arrangements of personal acquaintance and trust with impersonal financial facilities.[19] But the organization of the market for books was only an extension of the organization of the production of books, the control of production, of which "the publisher" was the specific form.

The "professionalization" of the writer may be seen as part of the same transformation of the relations of production, although again an understanding of the relationship is smothered by the free-enterprise epithet. For to posit a simple contrast between "aristocratic patronage and amateurism" on the one hand, and "professional writers" on the other,[20] is to make it impossible to see a transition from the forms of petty-commodity book production to those of a mature capitalism. That Byron and Scott had their doubts about authorship as a profession did not affect the historical change in writers' relationships to the literary mode of production, any more than did Dickens's unprecedented earnings, however much those may have helped make fiction-writing as professionally respectable as the law, medicine, or the civil service. The ideology of free enterprise, in particular the notion of the "profession," necessarily overlooks the new relationship of the writer to the new structures of publishing. When Constable, the publisher, insisted that every contributor to the *Edinburgh* was obliged to accept "a worthy wage," he may have, ideologically, "made the first move to dignify professional authorship by erasing the distinction between the gentleman amateur and the workaday writer and by cancelling the line between the Grub Street hack and the genius,"[21] but he certainly was recognizing, on the economic level, the place of the writer, genius or hack, in the relations of capitalist literary production, universalizing their labor-power rather than leveling up or down. The conventional accounts do not recognize the vulnerability of the writer in these new relations of production; dazzled by Dickens's £93,000 legacy, they can speak only of an author's new "independence" and "complete unaccountability," of how the "autonomous novelist," "his own man," "unfettered," communicates "the artist's awareness of his own power and the prime responsibility of looking after it."[22] Only this last phrase seems to acknowledge the precariousness of the writer's new position within the publishers' new structures for controlling the production of books. While the condition of early nineteenth-century writers never could decline to that of their wretched contemporaries, the hand-loom weavers, nevertheless Marx's comment on the weavers' predicament in the face of the new relations of industrial production is illuminating. Marx called attention to "the character of independence from and estrangement towards the worker, which the capitalist mode of production gives to the conditions of labour and the product of labour"; "free labour = latent pauperism," Marx wrote, and the writers' new professionalism concealed just such latencies.[23] If, in the late eighteenth century, "to a large extent the professional writer was the employee of the bookseller,"[24] with the "rise of the publisher" in the early nineteenth century, this dependency was changed and deepened. I shall return, later in this book, to the particular situation of the woman writer but here I want simply to point out that in general the writer, genius or hack, presented him- or herself to the publisher, as did any other worker in the capitalist mode of production, as "the owner of nothing but his labour-power,"[25] and so needed, as a "professional," to be "skilled and militant"[26] in the face of the publishers' new forms of "trade cooperation" and the new "sense of exclusiveness in trade affairs."[27] And the object of this new, necessary militancy was to be the literary text, newly defined as a commodity, newly available as the locus of surplus value.

John Sutherland says of publishing in the early decades of the nineteenth century that "it was not the book which was cheapened but the reading of it."[28] His distinction is that between a *book* and a *text,* precisely the distinction which had been made in the statutory law during the preceding century in the struggle over copyright, over the right to property in a text. Augustine Birrell described this long process as a controversy as to whether authors had a right to their published works "as *property* or as *privilege,*"[29] for previously the author's right to the text had only been recognized in the common law, and "copyright" had signified only a stationer's sole right to print and sell copies. "Property in literature was the right to make copies—not the right of authorship," and copyright was like "a perpetual lease of personal property . . . for one specific purpose, that of publishing."[30] It was only with the Statute of Anne (1709) that "the author in his own right appears on the scene"[31] and, more to our point, the rights to the "incorporeal property" in a work begin to be defined and established in statutory law. Whereas the Statute of Anne revoked the author's common law "perpetual" copyright and limited the initial period of copyright to fourteen years, authors could, for the first time, own the copyright of their work themselves. Indeed, the statutory copyright to "this amorphous property which increases so with technological progress" was now available to the author merely because it was now available to anyone; "the author could own the copyright only by virtue of the fact that anyone was now eligible to hold copyright."[32] This, I believe, is the significant historical point: with the Statute of Anne and the series of legal struggles and decisions culminating in the judgment in the Donaldson case in 1774, what had been a "continuing inchoate property," was redefined so that it might become a commodity like any other. As one historian puts it, "if the publisher is to profit, he must be able to acquire from the author an exclusive right—and so must the author be able to grant it," and so copyright came to be defined in law as "a monopoly of a work, rather than the basis of the monopoly of the book trade."[33] For the first time in statutory law there came to exist a property right in the text itself and that right was alienable. This was "precisely the kind of property," as C. B. Macpherson has shown, "that was required by a full capitalist market society": "a man's own labour, as well as capital and land, was made so much a private exclusive property as to be alienable, i.e., marketable."[34]

What I propose to label a "commodity-text" is such a text, produced in the new capitalist mode of production, produced in struggle by the new "professional" author within the new structures of control over the publishing process. These forms are, again, obscured in discussions, for example, of the kinds of agreements over the rights to their texts that writers signed with their publishers.[35] For what is at issue is not a straightforward matter of wages, royalties, or profits, as might be the case in a petty-commodity mode of production,[36] but rather the production of surplus value in a text, permitting high profits, and often high payments to the author. The term "commodity-text" thus indicates the text whose form, in Pierre Macherey's words "is not an initial datum, but a product, at the point where several lines of necessity converge."[37] Not a "structure" but a "structuration,"[38] a commodity-text is indeed "a differential network, a fabric of traces referring endlessly to something other than itself, to other differential traces,"[39] if we understand the traces to refer to the forces and relations of its production. The change in the understanding of copyright made it possible to imagine a commodity-text, just as the new forces and relations determined the limits of its possibility. Most importantly, the "fabric" of the commodity-text is "traced" by the mass bourgeois audience, for, while "specific literary works are determined by the history of literary production from which they receive the means of their own realization," so also readers are made by what makes the book:

> the book does not produce its readers by some mysterious power; the conditions that determine the production of the book also determine the forms of its communication. These two modifications are simultaneous and reciprocal.[40]

The commodity-text of the capitalist literary mode of production produces its readers by interpellating, that is, by addressing and engaging an infinity of bourgeois subjects,[41] "traced" in the text. These are the necessities determining the commodity-text, "the real diversity of elements which give it substance."[42] It realizes its surplus value in the ensemble of relations which structure its production and by its interpellation of a mass bourgeois audience; the concept commodity-text permits us to think of these processes as "simultaneous and reciprocal."

I shall return to my analysis of the historical processes, but I would first like briefly to describe more precisely in marxist terms how the commodity-text may be thought, by placing its production in relation to the general capitalist mode of production. The capitalist mode is characterized generally, as Gareth Stedman Jones says, "by a specific form of control over the labour process."[43] And so in the labor (or "creative") process of producing a commodity-text the specific form of control is series production. Whether the commodity-text is to take the particular form of a series of books, a magazine serial, or a part-issue novel, series production, by allowing the bourgeois audience's ideological engagement to be sensed and expanded, allows as well the extraction of ever greater surplus value from the very production (or "creative") process itself. The series writer in the capitalist mode, however the task may be perceived ideologically, must produce or discover in each successive book, or installment or part, that "virtually limitless multiplication" of ideological "inventions and combinations and configurations" which interpellate by constituting the bourgeois subject. This is not to be confused with writing to a "formula," for the audience we are describing is not "there," but rather always/already there: whereas a formula novel takes its value from something reduced and mechanical, and prior to its production, a commodity-text takes its value from the labor power ("imagination") expended in the very process of interpellation. Nor, on the other hand, does the simple category, "best seller," necessarily contain the concept commodity-text; "best seller" simply indicates value accrued through distribution and exchange, rather than through

9

the production process. The commodity-text, again, is produced by a writer within a determinate capitalist mode, a structure of specific means and relations of production, in which the series provides the distinctive form of control, and in which the profits are made by the ever more inevitable interpellation of a mass bourgeois audience.

Free-enterprise assumptions have shaped most accounts of the audience for books, implying that readers are brought together by their "reading habit" or their "appetite for fiction" into "the market-place," where publishers tempt them with their wares.[44] Or entrepreneurial publishers are said to have behaved as if they stood on a peak in Darien, "beholding for the first time a vast sea of common readers."[45] But two recent articles by Scott Bennett allow us to analyze the take-off period for the mass reading market[46] from the point of view of production, to see the audience as being made by what makes the book, rather than waiting to be "beheld." Bennett analyzes first the publishing project of John Murray's "Family Library" from 1829 to 1834, and he makes very clear the impossibility within the forms of petty-commodity book production—whose available and prospective market, as Hobsbawm said, "consists of the rich, who require luxury goods in small quantities, but with a high profit margin per sale"—even to "behold" what might constitute a mass audience. Murray, at the time London's most distinguished publisher,[47] introduced the Family Library as both an "early venture in the cheapening of books" and an "effort to publish across class lines at a time when class divisions were newly felt to be threatening the fabric of national life." The Family Library experiment was thus a publisher at once trying to create an audience and trying "to speak to the common reader in such a way as to heal the fundamental divisions created by the emerging industrial order." The experiment failed because "Murray was unable to translate the publishing practices of the market in which he had first established himself into the market for the common reader"; blocked in this way from producing a commodity-text by the forms of petty-commodity book production, Murray was equally, necessarily, unable to imagine how a text might interpellate a mass audience. His basic tactic was "to apply a brand name to a series of books and to rely on the general reputation of that name, as well as the individual books, to sell the series." At the same time his conservative political purpose was "to shape social attitudes through the use of literacy," to make his series "a vehicle for reuniting a dangerously divided society."[48] But neither his organization of production nor his conception of the text itself was adequate to the production of a commodity-text.

The project of the Society for the Diffusion of Useful Knowledge, however, as Bennett describes it, was radically different, marking "revolutions in thought" about the production of books and the relation to the audience. The SDUK, in conjunction with Charles Knight, combined the "conscious and innovative design" of sharply increasing the number of copies printed of its nonfictional publications to achieve a dramatically lower unit cost, and the idea of publishing serially, that is, to control the production process so as to lessen the attendant risks. At the same time the SDUK, unlike John Murray, approached "the issues of the day" indirectly: "as it matured in its purposes [the SDUK] was looking for a common ground in ideas and interests." Bennett suggests rightly that "the emergence of mass markets should stand alongside the emergence of class consciousness in our estimation of the new, most socially potent forces of the period." And since, as he says, "mass markets can exist only where widely shared interests or values exist or can be created," he explores the efforts of the SDUK to discover that common ground, that "common feeling, however partial it may be, in the day-to-day lives of the individuals who make up that market." What his study reveals is a stage in the structuration of the new mode of literary production, as Knight and the SDUK strive towards the possibility of a commodity-text. Their failure to achieve that "take-off" is less important historically than the fact that their project permitted "the clear emergence of fiction as the most saleable commodity on the market,"[49] for this conjuncture of capitalist control of the process of production with the emergence of the possibility of a commodity-text is the moment of transition into the specifically capitalist literary mode of production, just as it is (by no accident) the moment of *Pickwick*.

For *Pickwick Papers*, produced in the capitalist mode of production and drawing forth a mass bourgeois audience, was undeniably a commodity-text.[50] The production of *Pickwick* was, again, a complex process of structuration, and preoccupation with questions of genre and sources again blocks of perception of what Patten calls "the relationship in that novel of process to end."[51] While it has been claimed that *Pickwick* was "a highly derivative work . . . another example of a familiar and well-loved genre," or that the forerunners in *Pickwick*'s format "are found in two very different types of part-issue common in the eighteenth and early nineteenth century,"[52] the process by which it was produced, its literary mode of production, was original, as we can see by examining its specific historical determinations: Chapman and Hall can be recognized as the new publishers of industrial capitalism, just as Dickens can be seen as a free, professional writer and their mutual antagonistic struggle to produce a commodity-text analyzed as a whole process. *Pickwick Papers* was unique in Dickens's work "in being *begun* in response to an external demand;"[53] as Patten puts it, it "originated in the minds of others."[54] Moreover, because of the structures of capitalist publishing and because of prior discussions with Seymour, several crucial decisions had already been made when Dickens was recruited: "subject, relation of author to illustrator, publisher and format" were all predetermined.[55] The publishers' position in the enterprise was determined, of course, by their ownership of the means of production, but the other decisions affected those relations by which they would control the production process. The plan to publish in part-issue was undoubtedly the most crucial of these, for here an original combination of factors was being explored. For only in the late eighteen-thirties, that is, with the publication of *Pickwick Papers*, was the monthly part established as a method of publishing new fiction. *Pickwick* differed from its predecessors in one simple and all-important feature: "Chapman and Hall had *Pickwick* designed from the first as 1s. parts with a view to subsequent consolidation in volumes."[56] Whereas Chapman and Hall (and Seymour) might have been thinking at first in terms of yet another serial publication wedding hack text to humorous plates, that is, still thinking in terms of petty-commodity production, the particular relations of production which they and Dickens were to struggle over produced something qualitatively different from earlier serial publications. *Pickwick Papers* became something more than piecemeal publishing, which had merely made it "easy, for middle- and lower-class Englishmen to buy and read books;"[57] *Pickwick's* relations of production, its format, and its literary form constituted the very commodity-text which could reach, as it produced, a mass audience.

From the very beginning Dickens struggled with Chapman and Hall, and with the unfortunate Seymour, for control of the work process. There were disagreements, as we have seen, over the setting and over the balance of illustrations and text, and Seymour's views prevailed for the first few numbers.[58] In any form of serial publication, an author "ran the risk of subservience to editorial policy,"[59] but in the uncertainties following Seymour's death Dickens was able to take charge and to argue successfully for increasing the monthly text from twenty-four to thirty-two pages while decreasing the number of illustrations from four to two; thereafter, says Patten, "the author dictated all subjects and reviewed all designs, withholding approval until every detail satisfied him."[60] This did not mean that the struggle to produce a commodity-text was over, with the publishers raising Dickens's rate of payment and eventually presenting him with a £500 bonus.[61] Chapman and Hall had bought Dickens's intellectual labor power for nineteen months, divided into monthly intervals; the forms of control, initially imposed by capital and adjusted in the ways we have seen, determined that the "monthly something"[62] should be a discrete, illustrated, written text of a determinate length, produced regularly, and to be collected, complete, in a stated time. These details constituted the ideological form of the commodity-text: that each part was discrete, while yet a segment of a larger serial issue, allowed a focused, potent ideological apparatus; furthermore, the length of each written part demanded the development of setting, action, and characters "in richer detail and . . . somewhat greater roundness than hitherto."[63] Steven Marcus describes in another way the ideological effect of this aspect of the form of the text; the language of *Pickwick*, he says, "becomes capable of a constant, rapid, and virtually limitless multiplication of its own effects and forms in new inventions and combinations and configurations."[64] The expansion of the text, while itself perhaps not "virtually limitless," nonetheless produced just such an ideological effect of plenitude. Moreover, the ideological experience of *Pickwick* was to be regular and prolonged; as Dickens said in his announcement at the conclusion of Part 10, "we shall keep perpetually going on beginning again, regularly,"[65] and there was produced in this way "a close relation between author and reader," "the effect of contact," "a sense of long familiar association."[66] But the association was at the same time moving towards a promised and predictable close. Being more than just an indeterminate number of sketches, *Pickwick* anticipates its end, "discovers its shape,"[67] and moves towards becoming "a true whole, in which individual segments are subordinated to the totality of collective integration and collective affirmation."[68] Mr. Pickwick's "only" question, "where shall we go next?" (p. 578), is thus tempered by anticipation of the close, "in about twenty numbers."[69] These specific elements of the form of the commodity-text, determined as we have seen by the mode of production, themselves interpellate the multitude of bourgeois readers, allowing to each his own shilling number, prolonging while measuring the months of shared intimacy, and accumulating eventually into "that beloved Victorian thing, 'a cheap luxury.'"[70]

The ideologically shaped commodity-text had, as well, specific ideological content, achieved, again, in the struggles over its production. For example, the initial proposal from Chapman and Hall had been for "a book illustrative of manners and life in the Country,"[71] and the advertisement in the *Athenaeum* had promised travels over "the whole surface of Middlesex, a part of Surrey, a portion of Essex, and several square miles of Kent," penetrating even "to the very borders of Wales in the height of summer."[72] But Mr. Pickwick never makes it to "the fairs, regattas and market-days that were some of his original destinations," as Duane De Vries notes; "Instead, he keeps returning to London."[73] Or, more precisely, in the fourth number Mr. Pickwick returns to London, and from that point on, he was never really to leave it. This change from the original plan is crucial to the ideological content of *Pickwick Papers* because, as F. S. Schwarzbach points out, "as soon as Mr. Pickwick set foot again on the paving stones of a London street, *Pickwick Papers* sprang to life almost as if by magic." The "magic," we may add, is simply the ideological potential of that setting, for, as Schwarzbach mentions, "modern life is city life."[74] More specifically, ever since the industrial revolution the "urban realm" has become "the locus for the controlled reproduction of the social relations of capitalism,"[75] and *Pickwick Papers* is that process on the ideological level, its urban setting being one device interpellating the bourgeois subject of these social relations. The introduction into the story of that "living embodiment of London life,"[76] Sam Weller, in the fourth number presents a yet more complex ideological element. Terry Eagleton has called attention to the "corporatist forms assumed by bourgeois ideology" from the mid-nineteenth century onwards,[77] and I would suggest that the introduction of Sam Weller into *Pickwick Papers* and his relationship with Mr. Pickwick is an early instance of corporatist ideology. It is not just that "*Pickwick* cut safely across party lines," or that "all classes, in fact, read "'Boz,'"[78] but that "the affectionate communion" among Mr. Pickwick, Sam, and Tony Weller produces a determinate ideological effect by becoming the novel's principal focus of interest and by celebrating "the virtues of simplicity, innocence and directness in the relations of men." The portrayal of such a relationship between master and servant in 1836 (whatever its origin in Dickens's own experience) was a clearly ideological reading of "the revolution in public manners that took place in both the lower and middle classes during the eighteenth and the first quarter of the nineteenth centuries."[79] Thus the significance of the relationship between Mr. Pickwick and Sam lies less in its simple reproduction of the relationship between Don Quixote and Sancho Panza, than in its representation of an aspect of early Victorian England's way of seeing itself. For the implied parallel between Mr. Pickwick and Don Quixote (which "many readers must have detected"),[80] *together with* the difference in class and historical period, interpellate that specifically bourgeois Victorian sense of self. Acknowledging differences of status while blurring class antagonism, Pickwick's relationship with Sam incorporates that Pickwickian benevolence, which is "not so much *the matter of how* an individual preserves his better nature and finer instincts in a largely hostile or indifferent environment as *the assertion that* an individual can preserve his humanity under those circumstances."[81]

Finally, the gradual transformation, in the first five numbers, of the narration of *Pickwick* produces/is an effect of the ideological structuration of the commodity-text. This change has been noted often; Patten speaks, for example, of the alteration "from detached irony at Chatham to sympathetic identification in the Fleet and subsequently,"[82] and J. Hillis Miller's account might serve as a last example of the ways in which *Pickwick Papers* interpellates its mass audience:

> Bit by bit the distance and objectivity, with which the narrator at first watched Pickwick with ironic amusement, is replaced by sympathy and belief. This progressive destruction of a dry comic tone and its replacement by warmth and sympathy is, one might say, the hidden drama of the novel. What had been an interior play in which Dickens watched without sympathy another part of himself invent and enact the role of Pickwick becomes the mysterious attraction and domination of the author or narrator by his own creation. The narrator becomes fascinated by Pickwick, and, in the end, the narrator (and the reader) are wholly within the charmed circle of warmth and benevolence which derives from Pickwick and transforms everything around him. The reader and narrator, then, become believers in Pick-

wick, and, tempted to remain forever within his safe enclosure, we leave him reluctantly.[83]

Here Miller, like Steven Marcus commenting on the virtually limitless multiplication of *Pickwick*'s language, presents us with an ideological reading of the ideological effect of the text, his own prose measuring the process of interpellation, from "the narrator at first," through "the narrator (and the reader)" and "the reader and narrator," to "we." It remains to us outsiders simply to put a name, again, to that "charmed circle" of "believers."

Marcus comments that "Dickens was in no position to understand discursively what it was that he had done" in *Pickwick Papers*.[84] "Of course," he might well have added, as there was no such position available to anyone in 1836. Much of what Dickens had done in *Pickwick Papers* was beyond his understanding because it was out of his hands, produced by a set of forces and production relations whose historical determinations I have attempted to trace. What these structures (and Dickens) produced was a commodity-text with a determinate form, itself producing ideology, and the commodity-text, form, and ideology, creating the "wild and widespread enthusiasm"[85] of a mass bourgeois audience. "Whatever work is, in fact, produced," writes Edward Said, "is haunted by antecedence, difference, sameness and the future."[86] I have tried to recast descriptions such as this in materialist terms: the "hauntings," for *Pickwick Papers*, were not only "antecedent" genres but an obsolete literary mode of production; the "sameness" and "difference" imposed themselves in the struggle to establish the new. "The future," too, evokes no idealist form, but rather the historical form of the commodity-text. For the future, the new literary mode of production determined by the developing structures of Victorian capitalism, lay just there, in the ever more self-conscious, ever more assured exploitation of the surplus value of commodity-texts, within the dominant ideology of the commodity-book and the dominant economic structure in which it was embedded.

Two

Equipoise and the Three-Decker: The Production of *Henry Esmond*

It has been difficult for historians to characterize the mid-Victorian years, the 1850s and early 1860s, that period following the end of the Chartist struggles and fear of contagion from the Continental revolutions of 1848. "Victorian noon" or "the age of equipose"[1] convey metaphorically the sense of a pause but give no deeper sense of the dynamics of the pause, implying rather a suspension of dynamics, of historical forces, before new problems and new questions arise. The perceived equipose seems to deny what Trygve Tholfson, writing of the mid-Victorian city, has called "not only consensus and stability but unresolved ideological and social conflict: a stable culture in a state of inner tension."[2] Here I want to explore the inner tensions and conflicts, the structuring contradictions in the apparent equipoise of the early 1850s, within that specific sector of the social formation surrounding the production of novels, in particular the production of three-volume novels and of Thackeray's *Henry Esmond*. *Esmond* was the only one of Thackeray's novels originally produced as a three-decker and so it exposes in a complex but striking way the determinations of its production, what like other three-deckers it needed to be because of the specific relations of book production, its audience, and the ideological constraints of the historical moment. Thackeray finished writing *Henry Es-*

18

mond on 28 May 1852[3] and it happened that on that same day the Booksellers' Association disbanded, following the decision of a tribunal headed by Lord Campbell that the association's attempts to prevent other booksellers from discounting or "underselling" the established high book-prices were "harmful and vexatious," and inconsistent with principles of free trade.[4] We may approach an analysis of the publication of *Henry Esmond* through that particular episode, the Booksellers' Question of 1852, as an appropriate and symptomatically contradictory instance of "the lowering of social tension during the golden years of the mid-Victorians."[5]

The Booksellers' Question was ostensibly one phase in the struggle between different sectors of the London publishing world, between, that is, "the stalwarts of Paternoster Row, whose conservatism was something of a scandal in their own time," and "free traders," renegade booksellers like Bickers and Bush of Leicester Square, or John Chapman, the proprietor of the *Westminster Review*.[6] There had been in London an association of publishers and booksellers since 1829, brought together "to promote the solvency of the trade and the prosperity of literary speculations."[7] For the next two decades the executive committee of the association had, with varying success, enforced its regulations against undersellers by "trade ostracism," although "by the end of the 1830's there were unmistakeable signs of a mounting reaction against the bookselling restrictions,"[8] and in July 1850 the London booksellers decided to meet and to reaffirm the regulations of the trade. This was done, and the chief method of enforcing the restrictions against underselling was again to be publishers' boycott. But in 1852 the *Times* attacked the association in an editorial on "the free course of competition and the natural operations of trade" (*PPR*, 5), and John Chapman, who was being disciplined for selling American books at prices about 30 percent lower than those current, published in the *Westminster* a long, polemical analysis of "The Commerce of Literature." In the face of this publicity the Booksellers' Association decided to submit the issue to formal arbitration, the executive pledging itself to abide by the decision and to resign if the judgment were unfavorable, a pledge which came to mean the disbanding of the entire association. During the month which separated the two hearings of Lord Campbell's tribunal, Chapman and the undersellers put their case even more forcefully to the general public. On 4 May a public meeting of their supporters was held, chaired by Charles Dickens and attended by Wilkie Collins, F. W. Newman, and other prominent authors, at which were read statements of support from Carlyle, Gladstone, Mill, and Leigh Hunt. Also, John W. Parker, a London publisher, reprinted 100 letters from authors supporting free trade, including Carlyle, Darwin, Dickens, Mill, and Tennyson. These letters and the resolutions passed at the public meeting were forwarded to Lord Campbell, who presented his decision in favor of the "free traders" on 19 May; at the meeting on 28 May the Booksellers' Association was disbanded.[9]

To see this controversy as a sort of aftermath to Corn Law repeal, as an isolated struggle between "monopolists" and "free traders," is to skirt its real historical issues. James J. Barnes, in his extended study of the episode, acknowledges that "it has never been quite clear why the Association's Regulations had to be reiterated in July 1850" (p. 20). Understanding that decision is perhaps furthered by historicizing the event, by recognizing it as a moment in a larger historical struggle between two modes of literary production, the older, petty-commodity production of *books* being revolutionized by the capitalist production of *texts* made possible in part by new means of production (the eight-cylinder printing machine which Applegath and Cowper devised in 1848 was "one of the marvels of the Great Exhibition of 1851").[10] Lord Campbell wrote in his journal in 1848 of the effect on the sale of books of "turbulence," the Irish Famine, the repeal of the Corn Laws, the depression of 1847, and the political alarms of 1848,[11] and the actions of the Booksellers' Association were certainly intended to bring order again to the trade. But more significant by far was the kind of order which was restored, and how it differed from the order which had been disrupted. The Booksellers' Question was merely a symptom of the contradictions within the practices structuring book production in mid-century, and those may be read through the absences and silences in the ideological debate.

For if the Booksellers' Question is seen ideologically by modern historians ("it is possible, if rather fanciful, to conceive of the rebellion as somehow Oedipal"),[12] it was also, necessarily, seen ideologically by the participants, "stalwarts" and "free-traders" alike. Chapman inveighed against "indolent tradesmen of the 'old school'"[13] and Murray and Longman attacked "certain interested and ill-informed persons" (*PPR*, 8), and Gladstone told the House of Commons on 12 May 1852 that

> it has been the practice of the book trade to combine (I do not use the term offensively) against the public, and what is the consequence? . . . The natural and healthy play of the demand which ought to regulate the price, and of the principle that a book ought to sell for what it will fetch, neither more nor less, is totally intercepted by the system which has been so long in action. (*PPR*, 35–36)

John Murray, from the other side, defended this "inoffensive combination," which maintained high publishers' prices with discounts

> to enable the retailer to display the authors' and publishers' wares in expensive shops, to grant long credit, to pay carriage, to keep clerks and porters, and, above all, to speculate in the purchase of new books, with the risk of having them left on his shelves unsold. (*PPR*, 8)

Both tacitly acknowledge a dominating system, but the implications, it seems to me, go rather further than the simple to and fro of "a tension between innovation and a usually victorious entrenched conservatism";[14] they gesture instead towards discernible historical structures.

In the 1830s book publishers and booksellers had been "more involved in each other's spheres than was later to be the case";[15] indeed, publishing became "a separate and distinct trade from that of bookselling" only at about mid-century.[16] And the Booksellers' Question may, first of all, be seen to be an episode in that process of structural differentiation. But that historical process, which involved the development of the new means of production to which I have referred, was impeded by Gladstone's "system which has been so long in action." The contradiction mostly shows itself in the silent assumptions of both monopolists and free traders when they talk about the pricing of books. For what lurks behind the practices of the old-line booksellers is not simply a set of archaic pricing procedures or obsolescent marketing techniques but an ideological apparatus for market control. A letter to the *Times* makes clear the outlines of the controlled market for books. The writer, having come to London from a remote part of Scotland, protests against a system whose "sole effect . . . is to serve the extremities of the empire":

> We in London pay 10s. for a book, which we ought to get for 7s. 6d., that the publisher may sell the work at the same price in the Shetland Islands, or at Calcutta, or Sydney. (*PPR*, 28)

The unjust price he complains of is here clearly the symptomatic effect of a controlled, imperial market, and the structure of control is the real crux of the matter. The *Times'* editors made a similar allusion when on 29 May they pointed to "the original error of the publishers," that

> they have never forgotten to consider themselves booksellers too. They still think they are producing a book for the last purchaser instead of looking to their own immediate customer, the retail dealer. (*PPR*, 47)

Here the contradiction is very apparent between the new division of labor in publishing and a system of market control. Lecturing the old-line publishers on their distinction between "the trade price," set by costs, and the "publication price," which is 33 percent higher, the *Times* thundered against the publishers' casual assumption of the right to charge the extra 33 percent; this was a "monstrous wrong":

To assume that the publisher would be entitled
to this price in his own proper person if he did
not make "a reduction *in favour*" of the retailer, is
utterly preposterous. (*PPR*, 54–55)

Bickers, one of the undersellers, heartily concurred: "He
could not understand why a publisher should consider that
he was conferring a favour by selling a book.... For his own
part he had always been obliged to those who had pur-
chased books from him" (*PPR*, 39). These are the forms of
the struggle on the ideological level; personalized as the
"delusion or equivocation" (*PPR*, 54) of Longman or Murray, these assumptions are in fact both the ideological
perception and the ideological underpinning of the controlled market for books, the peculiar system which in itself, as a
system, is never clearly seen or challenged.

It is important to see how the controversialists might
allude to details of the controlled market yet never establish
a connection between that system and the matters of pricing
which they were debating; the visible details simply were
seen as too "natural" or "usual" to be questioned in that way.
Gladstone told the Commons on 13 May:

> You go into the houses of your friends, and,
> unless in the case of books for which they have a
> professional want that must be satisfied, or unless
> they happen to be persons of extraordinary
> wealth, you do not find copies of new publica-
> tions upon their tables, purchased for them-
> selves; but you find something from the circulat-
> ing library, or something from the book club.
> (Hear, hear). But, what are these book clubs and
> book societies, which are engaged, with such an
> enormous loss of time and waste of machinery, in
> the distribution of books throughout the coun-
> try? They are the ingenious expedients which,
> under the pressure of necessity, men have
> adopted to mitigate the monstrous evils they ex-
> perience from the enormously high price of
> books, and satisfy in some degree their own de-
> mand for that description of mental food. (*PPR*,
> 34–35)

Gladstone here misses the point that the high price is a component of a complex structure, as does Chapman when he asserts that novels were forced into "the publishers' Procrustean bed of three volumes post octavo" simply because the publishers know that "books of this class will be had at almost any price by the few."[17] Bickers misses the same point when, countering John Murray's argument about the necessary high expenses of bookshops, he says there is no need for expensive bookshops "with the exception of booksellers keeping circulating libraries" (*PPR*, 12). Bickers never questions his exception, nor does Gladstone do more than accept the fact of the existence of circulating libraries, just as Chapman accepts the existence of a wealthy few who can afford three-decker novels. None of them could recognize the articulation of high price, lending library, and the three-decker format as a hegemonic structure of market control, creating and sustaining a particular kind of readership, as it produced a particular kind of commodity with its own specific ideology.

Historians have often described the "kind of monopoly"[18] which existed in Victorian publishing, that

> publishers could afford to be indifferent to the fact that they had priced their wares out of the individual buyer's reach; so long as libraries took a substantial part of an edition, their profit was safe.[19]

The three-decker novel, "demanded by the circulating libraries, famously Mudie's," was "commercially safe," creating "a very benign state of affairs for the production of fiction."[20] But what needs to be emphasized is that this was more than a "state of affairs" which allowed fiction to be marketed profitably; rather it was a determinate hegemonic system, creating and controlling the kind of market to which alternative schemes (such as "free trade in books") necessarily had to accommodate. It was, and had been for two decades, the latest historical form of the dominant literary mode of production, the petty-commodity production of books, which had itself been "the established custom" as John Murray claimed, "of at least 100 years."[21] If the general mode of production in Victorian England was industrial capitalism, and the dominant ideology "free trade," there were as well sectors of the social formation still characterized by simple petty-commodity production, and in mid-century, publishing was one. Book publishing was marked by these contradictions; there were appearing various, more progressive, capitalist modes of literary production, such as part-issue and magazine serialization, but the dominant mode was the petty-commodity production of books which realized itself in that structure of high-priced three-deckers and libraries which we are examining, and in the attendant particular apparatuses and practices.

For example, the market for books was structured by a whole set of "traditional" discounts to booksellers, from the "normal trade allowance" of 25 percent to the cash discount of 2.5 percent and the prepublication "subscription" rate of 25 copies for the price of 24.[22] The book trade was characterized by the "agreeable custom" of publishers' dinner sales, with "speeches and toasts before the select company of the booksellers of London and Westminster were invited to say how many copies they would take of the publisher's new list."[23] Most of the new novels for sale were handled in large wholesale lots by jobbers, Simpkin, Marshall being the "central clearing house,"[24] but the bulk-buying of the libraries, particularly Mudie's, dominated the metropolitan market and a large portion of that in the country and overseas. In the process of "centralizing, cheapening and expanding service," writes Sutherland, "Mudie may be seen as literature's Rowland Hill,"[25] for although the circulating libraries in the provinces were clearly part of the structure,[26] everything tended to be centralized in London (and to a lesser extent Edinburgh).[27] Thus the close cooperation of publisher and library not only might ensure the commercial success of any three-decker, as did George Smith's promotional campaign for *Henry Esmond*, buttressed by Mudie's order of 430 copies,[28] but it also ensured a system of market control, of format and price, as well as of moral tone. The market control exhibited in the production of the three-decker novel was hegemonic, so that although the "free traders" of 1852 were able to defeat the efforts of Paternoster Row to exert a more overt disciplinary control, "free trade" was still to take place only within that still unchallenged controlled market; what might now be traded freely was still the three-volume novel required by Mudie and the old-time publishers.

For the dominant ideology of mid-Victorian publishing was that of the "commodity-book." The commodity which this whole system was constructed to produce was the *book* rather than the *text*, as various discussions of the three-decker make clear. Royal Gettmann, for instance, emphasizes how the three-decker was seen in the first instance as a physical thing; a novel was to consist of so many pages, so many lines per page, so many words per line, always in three volumes post octavo. These specifications were often detailed in contracts, but "writers who had any acquaintance with the ways of authorship must have known what was meant by 'the usual number of pages'." Thus contemporary guides and manuals for authors described "the average novel or romance" in this way, and reviewers spoke of the three-volume novel as if it were an exact thing with "a bulk of great amplitude that never varied."[29] Indeed, "bulk" is the word which perhaps best designates the fetishization of the commodity-book. The libraries' rationale for the three-volume format "was usually based on the argument that their subscribers were accustomed to value (i.e. bulk) for money"; as John Carter remarks, three-deckers were for those library patrons who "liked to feel they were getting their money's worth of reading,"[30] and A. W. Pollard refers to the "fixed idea that the more space a book occupies on a shelf the more money ought to be paid for it."[31] But the bulk of the three-volume novel was, of course, seldom referred to so directly; it was a "comforting bulk," as Guinevere Griest says,[32] and that spiritual comfort took various ideological forms. Not only were three-deckers "considered substantial by public and authors alike," but they had "prestige," "an aura of dignity and worth."[33] "For many in the nineteenth century," says Sutherland, "the three-volume novel had an inherited grandeur that could not be replaced."[34]

These are the ideological mediations of the commodity-book, for if the three-decker was "not simply a mercantile device, a way of packaging and pricing novels,"[35] it was nevertheless the product of a determinate historical structure, the petty-commodity literary mode of production of commodity-books, and we can now analyze that more precisely. The commodity-book constituted and was constituted by a particular, known sector of the bourgeois audience for fiction, that sector served by the lending libraries. It was a work manufactured for a certain market in both senses of the adjective. Griest discusses the themes and plots which the circulating-library reader preferred and she points out that "the middle- or upper-middle-class reader who exchanged his volume regularly under Mudie's dome received, besides entertainment, confirmation or definition of many of his beliefs."[36] And the "beliefs," the ideology of the consumer of the borrowed, three-volume commodity-book, were distinct from those of the consumer of the serialized or part-issue commodity-text. For whereas the commodity-text interpellated generally the individual bourgeois subject, the commodity-book was part of an apparatus which interpellated the "middle- or upper-middle class" subscriber to Mudie's. Mudie's subscribers were, in that small but significant way, an *exclusive* audience, having an exclusivity which might have been threatened by "free trade in books." Mudie's patrons were *subscribed* book readers, investing their subscription to Mudie's over a year's time. And thus, whereas the commodity-*text* interpellates the assumed "normality" or classlessness of the individual bourgeois subject/reader, the commodity-*book* interpellates in general the sense of an exclusive collectivity, as is implied by the "prestige" and "grandeur" associated with the three-decker. The Mudie's subscriber expected, in some heavily mediated way, such a "confirmation" of his or her exclusive status. The three-volume borrower, the consumer of the commodity-book, thus tended to be engaged, not by the experience of an adventurer/entrepreneur, a Pickwick, a Becky Sharp, or an Arthur Pendennis, but rather by an experience of belonging, as to a family, a faith, or a people, grounded, of course, in the real experience of belonging to Mudie's. It is to this ideological difference that Thackeray obscurely alludes when he writes to his mother that he had decided not to publish *Esmond* in numbers because "it's much too grave and sad for that."[37]

The History of Henry Esmond, which George Smith so assid-uously promoted in 1852, is thus a commodity-book, and not only because of the details of its "historical" pretense, the Queen Anne typeface and the deliberate archaisms. For the first time Thackeray chose to publish a novel not in shilling parts but in the three-volume format, and to do this he left Chapman and Hall and signed a contract with George Smith, of Smith, Elder, who had published his 1850 Christmas book, *The Kickleburys on the Rhine.* Thackeray had at this time made several personal decisions changing his life: he had broken with the Brookfields at the end of 1851, and he had judged it "best for my reputation" that he break his connection with *Punch* because of its cartoons lampoon-ing Palmerston and Louis Napoleon.[38] The move to Smith, Elder at that moment was also an ideologically revealing act. Smith, whom Charlotte Brontë judged "enterprising, yet cool and cautious,"[39] had been elected to the executive of the Booksellers' Association in 1850[40] and had supported the association's policy against "free trade"; Thackeray appears to have stayed clear of the controversy, neither attending meetings, sending letters, nor signing petitions, but in just those months he moved to George Smith and adopted a new format for his proposed novel. When Smith called on Thackeray to discuss the novel, Thackeray's daughter recalls her father saying in great excitement, "he has brought a thousand pounds in his pocket." But the "enterprising" publisher was nevertheless "cool and cau-tious," hedging in the eventual contract with terms which exercised "a necessary measure of tough disciplinary con-trol over the author," specifying delivery dates and dates of payment for "an original work of fiction, forming a con-tinuous narrative in three volumes post 8vo to consist of not less than One thousand pages of the usual novel size." Thackeray was here committing himself to producing the determinate commodity of petty-commodity book produc-tion. Smith brought to bear on the actual production of *Henry Esmond* none of the pressure attendant on part-publication; indeed "Thackeray was being paid by Smith to await inspiration."[41] But, as Edgar F. Harden points out:

> Thackeray was committing himself to a dual task he had never undertaken before—both completing a novel before publication and, by implication, working on it more or less exclusively.[42]

Although Thackeray may have conceived of it as "an artistic opportunity rather than a money spinner," *Esmond* was published in "the old pattern";[43] his contract and the three-volume format, "substantial, accepted, conventional,"[44] demanded from Thackeray a "complete work," marked by "wholeness and unity," indeed "in every sense, a book,"[45] including that sense we have labeled "commodity-book."

Henry Esmond interpellates its particular audience most obviously on the thematic level. Thirty years ago Gordon Ray described it as "a supreme example of the domestic novel, the dominant variety of fiction in the eighteen-fifties"; as "a chronicle of thirty-five years of life in a narrow family circle" and in its analysis of these "shifting relationships," *Esmond*, he says, is "primarily . . . a domestic drama."[46] Ray was preoccupied in *The Buried Life* with demonstrating how *Esmond* "reflects" Thackeray's relationship to Jane and William Brookfield, and he ignores how the novel places the domestic themes of filial devotion and loyalty into a pattern of loyalties, religious and political. Yet it is on that grander, historical terrain that Thackeray constructs the drama of *Henry Esmond*, which has, as Sutherland points out, "a 'crisis of loyalty' plot."[47] For on that broader social level, as on the domestic level, the questions raised are those of community and collectivity: what is it to belong? How is one true to "us"? Who are those others, whom we must not hate but who are nevertheless different? Thus, simply on the thematic level, *Henry Esmond* interpellates that specific bourgeois reader of three-decker fiction; or, as Gordon Ray puts it, *Esmond* re-presents "the gentlemanly ideal in a middle-class rather than an aristocratic context."[48]

But even on that simple thematic level the loyalties which the novel explores are vexed and contradictory. Writing in

Virginia in later life, the aging Henry Esmond describes
English history as "a strange series of compromises": "compromise of principle, compromise of party, compromise of
worship."[49] In England, he says, "you take the house you live
in with all its encumbrances, its retainers, its antique discom-
forts, and ruins even; you patch up but you never build up
anew," and he wonders for how much longer the North
American colonies will submit, even nominally, to "this
ancient British superstition" (373). This, too, is thematically
significant, for all the loyalties on which the novel settles are
beset with compromise. Esmond, for example, compromises in various ways in his loyalties, religious, political, and
domestic, and the novel continually "worries" the matter of
loyalty to a group or cause ("one's own") with the possibility
of compromise and, dangerously, the threat of what is
called, in the British political tradition, "trimming."[50] Indeed, the novel poses "trimming" rather than simple infi-
delity as the great threat to loyalty. The text encompasses
not only the "bent of mind" of Tom Tusher, "always per-
fectly good-humored, obliging and servile" (110) but more
subtly Father Holt's lectures to the young Esmond on the
theological doctrine of "Reserve," "all which instruction . . .
the boy took eagerly and with gratitude from his tutor" (49).
The loyalties of the middle-class gentleman must be poised
and accommodating, must admit *some* compromise (the
compromise of "exclusivity" by "entry," for example) and
Thackeray attempts, in his novel "without any villain" (*LPP*,
II, 736), to display this balance against the "trimmers,"
Tusher, Holt, and especially the Duke of Marlborough.

For, villain or not, Marlborough, as Sutherland has re-
marked, "overshadows the second and third books as
Esmond's *bête noir*."[51] Thackeray appears to have accepted
wholeheartedly Macaulay's description of Marlborough's
besetting avarice, in fact adding to it judgments which were
even harsher than Macaulay's.[52] Marlborough was "a
mercenary traitor,"[53] he wrote in the unpublished appendix
to Book II, and from the first, says Sutherland, Thackeray
seems to have been fascinated not only by Marlborough's
avarice but by his perceived duplicity.[54] The Snows, in the
Biographical Appendix to their edition of *Henry Esmond*, say

in "palliation" of Thackeray's view that "double-dealing between the Stuarts and their rivals was the common practice of the times" (572), but Thackeray was convinced of Marlborough's exceptional duplicity; in his lecture on Richard Steele in *The English Humourists*, he had spoken of Marlborough's "secret motive" (avarice, perhaps), but had emphasized how it had "caused his turnings and windings, his opportune fidelity and treason . . . and landed him finally on the Hanoverian side—the winning side."⁵⁵ What Thackeray foregrounds, here as in *Henry Esmond*, is the opportunistic "trimming" by which the "ambidextrous Churchill" (423) was thought to have shaped his career and against which the special loyalty of Esmond might be understood.

But compromise and duplicity are not merely thematic issues in *Henry Esmond;* they shape the novel on the level of its narration, marking the text with the contradictions in its literary mode of production. What Gordon Ray has called Thackeray's own "characteristic doubleness"⁵⁶ manifests itself in the text in peculiar forms because of the demands of his contract with George Smith, and of the three-volume format and Mudie's. A formulation of Thackeray's "doubleness" has often been used to explain the ambivalences in his fiction, the role of the narrator in *Vanity Fair*, for example, presenting an "ambivalent," or "oblique," "version of the novelist's responsibility."⁵⁷ Ann Y. Wilkinson, in an acute essay, has analyzed the precise mediations of this obliquity in *Vanity Fair*, showing that the way of knowing which informs its narration is the way of *gossip*, "which consists in knowing the secrets, especially the discreditable ones, of great men, and in 'giving them credit' . . . on the basis of this secret knowledge."⁵⁸ The narrator of *Vanity Fair* is, simply, "a gossip who is telling a story he has gleaned largely through gossiping with other eavesdroppers," and our participation in the "Tomeavesian" world of *Vanity Fair* is therefore

> that of accomplices to a master eavesdropper, as opposed, say, to the direct, dramatic participation in the world of Dickens' novels, or the reflective, philosophically grounded participation in the world of George Eliot's novels.⁵⁹

The first point to be made is that Thackeray "domesticates" this rakish narrative mode for his three-decker novel; the narrator there is Henry Esmond, telling his own story, with footnoted comments from time to time by his wife, his grandson, and by his daughter, who edits his memoirs sixty years later. But "Tom Eaves," the arch-gossip of *Vanity Fair*, "who has no part in this history, except that he knew all the great folks of London, and the stories and mysteries of each family,"[60] has indeed a part in the history of Henry Esmond. He is accommodated to the decorum of the three-decker novel as Father Holt, and his narrative function is transformed, his way of knowing reined in somewhat, gossip becoming "Jesuitry." While neither "infallible nor divine" (268), Holt, like "Tom Eaves," knows the truths that others can only guess at: he reveals the facts of Henry's birth to his protector, Francis Esmond (194), having learned them from the third viscount's confessor after the Battle of the Boyne (185-86); he knows the later history of Esmond's mother (194), and is able to show him her birthplace (273) and her grave (277). Thus Holt, as a dramatic character, accommodates the "Tomeavesian way of knowing" to *Henry Esmond*, moderating the duplicity of the oblique narrator of *Vanity Fair* while yet making known information which is realistically accessible in no other way. The quality of our participation, in Wilkinson's phrase, no longer need be that of "accomplices to an eavesdropper"; we simply learn, along with Esmond, from his old tutor, for whom "in the cause of religion and loyalty all disguises are fair" (272).

Henry Esmond, as we have seen, was necessarily to be produced as a complete work, marked by wholeness and unity, and Father Holt's special knowledge is crucial to the plot which unifies the novel. Those very details which are to enforce the unity required in a three-decker, however, produced the contradictions which expose its ideological basis. Holt carries the knowledge of Esmond's legitimacy, and it is crucial to the plot of *Henry Esmond* that, besides this priest, only Esmond and the reader (except for the dowager viscountess, who is peripheral to the main plot) should share this knowledge, and, furthermore, that Esmond and the reader should know early, by the end of Book I. Book II

begins, significantly, with the sequence of Lady Castlewood's grief-stricken reproach to Esmond, then Tom
Tusher's hypocritical letter communicating Esmond's
banishment from her presence, and then Esmond's tor-
tured response to this injustice (167–72). The significance
of these details lies in how they distance Esmond from
Rachel, in the story and in the reader's expectations. The
possibility of a marriage between the two is at this point in
the novel being forcefully and systematically occluded. But
the most powerful guarantee that the reader be diverted
from that possibility is the narrative use made of the knowledge of Esmond's legitimacy. Although Esmond burns the
Viscount Castlewood's deathbed revelation so as not to
bring "double misfortune on those he loved best" (162), the
effect of his decision is to encourage the reader to anticipate
Esmond's eventual marriage to Beatrix. At any moment, as
we know, Esmond is able to reveal his legitimate birth, to
claim his true rank and family status, and thus to remove the
main obstacle to his suit. His self-imposed, self-defined
"loyalty," however "right" it might seem to the Victorian
reader, is thus also a plot device, maintaining the expecta-
tion of a particular ending.

Thackeray's portrayal of James Edward, which the
Snows labeled "the greatest historical mistake in *Esmond*"
(569), is the necessary complementary narrative element to
the secret knowledge of Esmond's legitimacy. The Cheva-
lier de Saint George

> was not at any time of his life Thackeray's spoiled
> and charming and slippery and self-indulgent
> boy, but, almost from the beginning, grave
> beyond his years, unexpansive and disappoint-
> ing in social life, anxious and conscientious and
> ineffectual. (569–70)

But if the historical James was "conspicuously not a libertine" (570), the fictional purposes of *Henry Esmond* required
a conspicuous high-born libertine who, while forestalling
Esmond's courtship of Beatrix, nevertheless cannot marry
her, as the tantalized Mudie's reader would know, as much
from "experience" as from "History." Which is not to say

33

that in the end a "mistake" was not made, since the very library reader whose conventional attitudes might be manipulated in these ways to anticipate Esmond's marriage to Beatrix was the same reader who was very disturbed when the actual working out of Esmond's life, however cleverly it was prepared, violated other conventions, ones with a powerful ideological charge.

For if on the level of plot and character the necessary elements are the "illegitimate" Esmond's known legitimacy and James Edward's unhistorical libertinism, the direction in which they shape the plot produces the novel's unforeseen major contradiction, which exposes the very ideology of its production. For in concealing the facts of Esmond's birth and encouraging anticipation of his marrying Beatrix, Thackeray produces Esmond's relationship as dependant and confidant, as "son," to Rachel. This is the ultimate effect of Esmond's self-defined loyalty to his benefactors. The "rude picture representing Jacob in hairy gloves, cheating Isaac of Esau's birthright," which overlooks the death of Viscount Castlewood (162) suggests an analogy which is too finely drawn; Esmond is *not* Frank's brother, nor is he Rachel's son, although the exigencies of plotting constantly place him there. Drawing no doubt on Thackeray's sense of his own "loyal" negotiation of the difficulties in his marital position, and in particular of his very carefully constructed relation as "brother" (*LPP*, II, 680, 689, 709) to Jane Brookfield, the correlative position of "loyal son" in Thackeray's novel, when Esmond achieves a fulfillment not available to Thackeray himself, produces the imputation of "incest," and bourgeois moralism pronounces against what is the creation of bourgeois moralism. Thackeray is not, in my opinion, playing with an incest fantasy, as Sylvia Manning argues.[61] Rather, his fictional exploitation, for his new audience, of elements of his own authorial ideology of loyal gentlemanliness produces an intimation to which that same more uniformly domestic bourgeois audience can react only with great unease. And this, the major contradiction in *Henry Esmond,* is as well the major imprint on the novel of its literary mode of production.

For the three-volume format, and the commodity-form

specific to that mode of production, necessitated a relatively more unified whole ("in every sense a book"). Our greater attention to thematic elements of that whole is similarly necessitated by *Henry Esmond*'s production as a commodity-book, of which bourgeois moralism is a distinctively intrusive ideological determination. The themes and issues of his life, as the older Esmond presents them in his quaint Queen Anne English, interpellate the particular ideology of the three-decker readership, patrons of the circulating library, that other constituent element of petty-commodity book production. The peculiar articulation of these same intricacies, the "gentlemanly" behavior which, ironically, predetermines the intimation of incest, interpellates that same readership; and these determinate features of the production of *Henry Esmond*, the necessary unity and the particular interpellations, together produce the "ideology of the text"[62] with its salient contradiction, registered since its first publication in the disquiet of its readers.[63] The elements which constitute the mode of production display themselves in the contradictory tension of *Henry Esmond*, and the system which the mode of production *is*, becomes apparent in that silent distortion, just as it became apparent in the awkward silences in the pronouncements of Gladstone, Chapman, and John Murray, as they sought within the system's silent "equipoise" to justify their different schemes for the production of books.

Three

One Round of a Long Ladder: Gender, Profession, and the Production of *Middlemarch*

On 7 May 1871 George Henry Lewes wrote to John Blackwood, George Eliot's publisher, inviting him to "run down and see us," and mentioning as well "something for you to turn over in your mind, and come prepared to discuss." George Eliot had begun "experimenting in a story" six months earlier, and by March she was worrying that she had too many "momenti." Lewes's letter to Blackwood in May was to ask him to turn over in his mind an experiment in publishing format:

> Mrs. Lewes finds that she will require 4 volumes for her story, not 3. I winced at the idea at first, but the story must not be spoiled for want of space, and as you have more than once spoken of the desirability of inventing some mode of circumventing the Libraries and making the public *buy* instead of borrowing I have devised the following scheme, . . .—namely to publish it in *half-volume parts* either at intervals of one, or as I think better, two months. The eight parts at 5/- could yield the 2£ for the four volumes, and at two month intervals would not be dearer than Maga [*Blackwood's Magazine*]. Each part would have a certain unity and completeness in itself with separate title. Thus the work is called *Middlemarch*. Part I will be *Miss Brooke*.[1]

Lewes's scheme, which was indeed to set the format for the publication of *Middlemarch*, has been discussed in several places,[2] as has the actual composition of the novel, which had begun in 1869, not as "Miss Brooke" but as "Middlemarch."[3] Leaving aside for the moment the matter of its composition, I should like to examine historically the question of the novel's publication, and its apparently "exotic"[4] relation to the dominant literary mode of production.

For to see Lewes's new publishing format simply as a change in "sales strategy" or a "hybrid" of fiction-for-buying and fiction-for-lending which would "cream both markets," is, again, radically to dehistoricize the production of *Middlemarch*, to place it only as an "acute form" of a "perennial struggle." In the standard accounts the historical context for publishing in the late 1860s and early 70s is surprisingly vague: "it was clear that the circulating libraries were in their decline," or "it was felt that the traditional forms like the three-volume novel and the monthly thirty-two-page serial had had their day."[5] But the dominant structure in publishing, that special relationship between the advertised high price of novels, the three-volume format, and the lending libraries, was to persist until the 1890s, and a materialist account of the appearance of the *Middlemarch* format would need to ground itself in more specific historical details than that of a vogue which might have "had its day." Nor is it any more useful to derive the new format from an ingenuity or "excessive greed" imputed to Lewes and George Eliot;[6] our purposes are better served on the analytical level by seeing "Lewes" and "George Eliot" in structural terms, as in Terry Eagleton's formulation, as "nothing more than the insertion of certain specific ideological determinations"—among them an "incipient feminism"—"into a hegemonic ideological formation, which is partly supported, partly embarrassed by their presence."[7] A more dialectical and historically specific analysis of the production of *Middlemarch*, then, might want to examine the determinate relation of those "authorial" determinations, "gender" being crucial, to that structured literary mode of production, finding in their interplay an explanation for

37

this "exotic" new format. At their most abstract our questions would be:

> what are the forms taken by patriarchy in this society, and how are they interrelated with the social relations of production? How, in other words, do changing modes of production change the forms of patriarchy without destroying its existence?[8]

These abstract questions about the forms of patriarchy in general may be grounded in the growing body of empirical work on the rise of the nineteenth-century women's movement. These historical studies examine not only the legal benchmarks of reform (the Infant Custody Act [1839], the Marriage and Divorce Act [1857], the opposition to the Contagious Diseases Acts of the 1860s and the Married Women's Property Act [1870]) but also the struggles of individual women, Caroline Norton from 1836, or Barbara Leigh Smith's *Brief Summary in Plain Language of the Most Important Laws Concerning Women* (1854), and the struggles of women collectively, the founding of the *English Woman's Journal* (1858) and the Society for the Employment of Women (1859–60), and the "Ladies' Petition" on suffrage to the House of Commons in 1866.[9] These struggles and others display what Bessie Rayner Parkes called "the material need which exerted a constant pressure over a large and educated class,"[10] a group including women writers. My approach to George Eliot's situation as a woman writer will be to analyze the specific forms of pressure on it exerted by her particular woman's material need, rather than examining her friendships with Parkes or Barbara Bodichon, or the degree of her involvement in the *English Woman's Journal,* the "Ladies' Petition," or the founding of Girton College.[11] While patriarchal relations are relatively autonomous within the capitalist social formation, by exploring the specifics of their operations in the situation of a woman writer we may see how "the articulation of an individual's work to the social relations of a given mode of production determine how she is related and the ways in which she becomes subordinate."[12]

Juliet Mitchell has proposed a way of analyzing woman's situation as "a *specific* structure, which is a unity of different elements":

> The key structures of woman's situation can be listed as follows: Production, Reproduction, Sexuality and the Socialization of Children. The concrete combination of these produces the "complex unity" of her position; but each separate structure may have reached a different "moment" at any given historical time. Each then must be examined separately in order to see what the present unity is.[13]

Such Acts, actions, and movements in mid-Victorian England as I have listed, engaging property relations and the opportunities for work, marriage relations and their dissolution, the control of female sexuality and the custody of children, electoral political change and suffrage, these "several structures" of production, reproduction, sexuality, and socialization, "moving at different paces," constitute historically that "overdetermined unity," Victorian woman's situation.[14] Marian Evans's specific place within that structured unity was contradictory; it was not that (as Kate Millett says) " 'living in sin,' George Eliot lived the revolution,"[15] but rather that to control her own reproductive function, as she did, to express her own sexuality, variously to support the children of Agnes Lewes, *and* to live, herself, as "Mrs. Lewes" in a high bourgeois fashion, was to live in intense, willed contradiction.[16] For legally Marian Evans was "feme sole," the term for the "single woman of mature age" whom English law put "on practically a par with men so far as private rights are concerned."[17] While deprived of the "protection and benefit" of the law for married women ("so great a favourite is the female sex of the laws of England"[18] that this was in the 1860s and 70s primarily a right to maintenance), as a single woman Marian Evans had complete control over her own property, complete power to enter into legal contracts, and a liability for debts identical with any man's, say that of G. H. Lewes.[19] George Eliot's relation as a writer to the structure of literary production was thus overdetermined by the contradictory unity of the other three structures of her situation as a Victorian woman.

Indeed, adapting Eagleton's phrase, I have been using "George Eliot" to signify only Marian Evans's determinate relation to the literary mode of production. That pseudonym, rather than being "a complicated way of dealing with the question of origin," turning Marian Evans into "George Eliot, the offspring of her own work, her own imagination,"[20] instead marks the very specificity of her structured position as a Victorian woman writer. It specifies the effect of social coercion enforcing feminine subordination on the level of production, to some extent "ameliorated" in the sphere of literary production to "an ideology shared by both sexes." Not all the forms of that patriarchal ideology in book production have, I think, been located, for literary critical practice often occludes them. In "The Sociology of Authorship" in 1962, Richard Altick argued that "clearly the broadening opportunities in the field of letters had little effect on women during the nineteenth century, because of the inadequate educational provisions, and the persisting prejudice against careers for females."[21] But the phrase, "persisting prejudice," so simply stated, allows us to ignore the fact that the prejudice persisted because it was embodied in material practices. Gaye Tuchman and Nina Fortin have recently demonstrated in detail how women were "frequently excluded from the social network central to cultural milieus," for example, the network of readers and editors of the large publishing houses.[22] The constant pressure to which women writers were subjected had a more material force than "persistent prejudice" implies, just as more was being denied them than straightforward "careers" in "the field of letters."

For the capitalist middle class, "the career . . . structures the entry and activity of the individual as economic agent."[23] As John Stuart Mill observed in *The Subjection of Women*, not only did their sex constitute for all women "a peremptory exclusion from almost all honourable occupations," but what social institutions were open did not "admit the same free development of originality in women which is possible to men." The institutional exclusion in the arts, moreover, had a determinate ideological effect:

> Women in the educated classes are almost universally taught more or less of some branch or other of the fine arts, but not that they may gain their living or their social consequence by it. Women artists are all amateurs.

Women artists are all amateurs; Mill emphasizes that this is a social fact, that the theater (the "histrionic") is the only art which women may follow "as a profession and an occupation for life,"[24] and we might examine for a moment just how the ideological opposition, "amateur/professional," organized Victorian middle-class occupations to the exclusion of women. For as "professionalization" coincided with "the rise of industrial capitalism . . . and . . . with the evolution of capitalism toward its corporate form,"[25] so the distinction "amateur/professional" was historically a crucial development of bourgeois ideology. The modern uses of the terms, as opposites, arose in the early nineteenth century: "amateur," as "one who cultivates anything as a pastime, as distinguished from one who presents it professionally," first recorded in 1803, and "professional," used in contrast to "amateur," first recorded in 1805. Each term not only defined itself as a positive value against the other, but apparently from the beginning each also might itself be used disparagingly, "amateur" for a dabbler or a superficial worker, and "professional" for "one who 'makes a trade' of anything that is properly pursued from higher motives" (*OED*). This radical relativity on the level of the signified indicates the extent to which "amateur" and "professional" were ideological counters in the processes of social coercion through which sectors of the bourgeoisie relentlessly pursued income security and social respectability.[26] And this is the ideological terrain on which we can begin to locate both Mill's perception of women's peremptory exclusion from "honourable occupations" in general and Marian Evans's practice as a woman artist. Here we may see how "George Eliot" might be said to be, in the strictest sense, her *professional* name.

It is important to insist that "amateur" and "professional" are not static categories but constitute a field of ideological tension. At the core of the historical process of "professionalization"—the "professional project"—was "a fusion of antithetical ideological structures"; the concept, professionalization, does not refer to "the goals and strategies of a given group" in nineteenth-century England, but rather to "the coherence and consistence that can be discovered ex post facto in a variety of apparently unconnected acts."[27] For while the Victorian age was, indeed, "the key period for the emergence and consolidation of the leading professions, and for the crystallization of the professional ideal as a separate entity, increasingly critical of the entrepreneurial,"[28] that "crystallization" must be seen dialectically, as a particular, ideological instance of "the general growth of semi-private institutions where rules of selectivity would guarantee social acceptability."[29] One literary historian would use the term "professional" to distinguish "those like Southey who worked for high ideals, from those hacks and compilers whose aim was merely the day's wage,"[30] but so to conflate "profession" with "vocation," or to use it as a synonym for "occupation," employing "participation in the labour market as its essential function," is to employ a "folk concept."[31] Instead, within a generic conception of occupations, "professionalization" can be used "to order and guide the explanation of the circumstances of a variety of historical occupations," the processes through which they "develop, maintain themselves, grow and decline."[32] From this point of view, sociologists of professions have examined the development of criteria of special knowledge, formal higher education, and skill, and especially that distinctive feature of professions,

> the degree to which they, as occupations rather than classes, have gained the organized power to control themselves the terms, conditions and content of their work in the settings where they perform their work.[33]

The specific ideological practice of strict professions is to secure "a labour monopoly and a place in the division of labour that is free of the authority of others over their work"; the professional project is an organizational project, tending toward "the monopolization of status and work privileges."[34] Its ideological form is "vocation," the commitment to a particular occupation, or kind of work, and solidarity with others so committed, as well as commitment to one's own work in the chosen occupation. These two dimensions, the antithetical ideological structures of labor monopoly and vocational commitment, fuse in the professional project to form "the specifically bourgeois economic ethic," generating tensions not only for the profession as a whole but for the individual professional. For this fusion of the vocational and the entrepreneurial is intensely individual and personal:

> Unlike craft or industrial labour, . . . most professions produce intangible goods: their product, in other words, is only formally alienable and is inextricably bound to the person and the personality of the producer. It follows, therefore, that *the producers themselves have to be produced* if their products or commodities are to be given a distinctive form.[35]

Thus, a central focus in the analysis of professionalism becomes not only "the role of the title ["professional"] in the aspirations and fortunes of those occupations claiming it,"[36] but the role of that title in the aspirations and fortunes of those individual producers who produce themselves as professionals.

It is in this historical context that "George Eliot" may be seen as Marian Evans's "professional" name. It marks the articulation of her work to the social relations of the literary mode of production, and in the difference between a professional *name* and a professional *title* lies the determinate influence of gender distinctions on the professional project. For to see professionalism historically, as a project of occupational organization to the exclusion, among others, of women as a group, is to escape the individualist idealism which mars Elaine Showalter's account of the first, "feminine" generation of "professional" women writers, which she dates "from the appearance of the male pseudonym in the 1840s to the death of George Eliot in 1880." Showalter sees the appearance of the male pseudonym as "one of the many indications that this generation saw the will to write as a vocation in direct conflict with their status as women,"[37] but her analysis is distorted by her use of the "folk concept" of "profession," reducing it to "occupation" and "vocation." Not that George Eliot, for example, did not herself share this position, urging woman writers in 1856 "to prove that they are capable of accurate thought, severe study, and continuous self-command."[38] But by 1870 George Eliot also to some extent knew the organizational structuring of at least one profession, medicine, whether or not she fully realized that its organizational ideological practices were historical mediations of the status of women, whatever their self-command or will to write. For while mid-Victorian literary professionalism had not yet arrived at the definition of status marked by the founding of the Society of Authors in 1884 (nor did it, of course, ever achieve the organized control of the terms, conditions, content, and settings of work which characterizes modern medicine), nevertheless writers, like other bourgeois occupational groups, were engaged in their own professional project, of which the founding of the Society of Authors, and *The Author* in 1890, are only climactic moments. As writers collectively moved towards such occupational organization as these represented, individual writers struggled over status on the ideological terrain of the "folk concept" of professionalism, as John Stuart Mill implied in 1869. For while writing might offer "unique financial opportunities without sex discrimination" in the 1850s,[39] women artists were still "all amateurs." And if in the 1840s "fiction-writing became a viable male profession," 1887 was "a benchmark in the process of edging women out."[40] Ideologically speaking, that process was the professionalization of authorship; "woman writer" and "professional" were constructed as contradictory concepts, the hard truth being, as Elaine Showalter remarks, "that 'authoress' was a term and a category capacious enough to accommodate them all."[41]

Showalter asserts that George Eliot, annoyed that, "in the

eyes of male critics the intellectual differences between her books and those of lesser talents were canceled out by the fact of their shared womanhood," went on to "meet, and to set, a high standard of female literary professionalism."[42] Again, this sees "profession" in idealist terms, ahistorical and independent of gender, a matter of "career patterns" and the vocational will-to-write,[43] rather than embedded in gender-determined ideological practices. For while it might appear that "George Eliot earned her reputation on the grounds she chose," she necessarily chose the grounds which were already there; George Eliot, like the rest of us, made her own history, but she did not make it just as she pleased.[44] The interplay of the vocation of author and the situation of women on the terrain of professionalization (and within a dominant literary mode of production) produced that "material need which exerted a constant pressure" on George Eliot. Bessie Parkes had written to her in 1858 to ask her to contribute to the *English Woman's Journal* and she had refused:

> My negative about the writing has no special relation to the "Englishwoman's Journal". . . . I have given up writing "articles," having discovered that my vocation lies in other paths. In fact *entre nous*, I expect to be writing *books* from some time to come. . . . It is a question whether I shall give up building my own house to go and help in the building of my neighbor's garden wall.[45]

Her task was, in fact, to gain the status and the organized power of a professional, as a woman and with so individualist a sense of vocation, to control the terms, conditions, and content of her work, in the settings where she performed her work.

It is in the details of George Eliot's publishing practice that we may best read, symptomatically, the struggle between her vocation, her will to be a professional, and the dominant, patriarchal structures of professional authorship and publishing, "symptomatically" because to read her practice simply as the demonstration of her indeterminate "business sense" and Blackwoods' "tactful, forbearing and

generous" response is again to dehistoricize the relations of
production of her novels and to entertain Blackwoods' private speculations about her "mercenary trait."[46] The publication history of George Eliot's novels is usually presented
from an individualist, capitalist, and masculinist perspective, but while we may acknowledge that "no publisher
could have been more assiduous than John Blackwood in
his attentions to George Eliot,"[47] we may at the same time
want to emphasize that these are the attentions of a male
capitalist towards a "feme sole," the surplus value of whose
intellectual labor produces his profits. We should notice the
other effects of that production relation which are obscured
by a preoccupation with Blackwoods' generosity. For example, negotiations for *The Mill on the Floss* took place during
1859 in the months immediately following the publication
and immense success of *Adam Bede,* whose copyright for
four years George Eliot had sold to Blackwoods for £800.
One can understand very well, especially if one underscores
that the £800 was George Eliot's "*contracted* payment," why
Blackwoods were disappointed at the "tart tone and terse-
ness" with which she accepted two subsequent £400
bonuses, her "greater-than-contracted-for share in the success of *Adam Bede.*" Such a point of view, capitalist and male,
necessarily predetermines that the "logic" of George Eliot's
response was "untenable,"[48] but we may insist on the con-
trary, that George Eliot, like other women workers, had
good reason to be "ever anxious about money and securing
it," reasons other than the "insatiable greed" attributed to
her by one Blackwoods advisor or the "feminine" suscepti-
bility to Lewes's influence assumed by the Blackwood
patriarchs.[49] One can see instead in these negotiations the
signs of an incipient professional project. For besides her
general anxieties as a woman author selling her intellectual
labor power, George Eliot was concerned specifically with
the relations of production in her work. Her regret at having sold the copyright to *Adam Bede,* a petty-commodity
production relation, is directly related to her desire—when
she inferred that John Blackwood saw her next book as "a
speculation attended with risk"—to change the relations of
production by contracting only for the first edition of *The*

Mill: "I prefer incurring that risk myself."[50] Her disagreements with John Blackwood inevitably return to the links between format and sales, and it is at this time, during the negotiations over *The Mill on the Floss,* that Lewes first mentions to John Blackwood the possibility of its publication in shilling numbers, a plan opposed by Blackwood and by George Eliot herself.[51]

But it is in the negotiations for *Romola* that the constant pressure of George Eliot's professional vocation first makes itself clearly felt; "a sense of her work as part of a 'career' coalesced at this time."[52] The struggle over the relations of production again can easily be obscured by a readiness to see the cause of the tension as her "marked keenness in money matters," her "lack of confidence in John Blackwood's business integrity" or even "the snipings of a passive-aggressive personality," or, again, to suspect that Lewes is "the villain of the piece."[53] From the start George Eliot saw the format of *Romola,* a historical romance so different from her earlier work, as a way of advancing her professional project. She proposed in August 1860 that it first appear anonymously in *Maga,* following quickly on *Silas Marner,* which was to come out in volumes, then to reprint *Romola* in volumes as by "George Eliot." She confided to John Blackwood,

> I need not tell you the wherefore of this plan—
> you know well enough the received phrases with
> which a writer is greeted when he does some-
> thing else than what was expected of him,[54]

and the masculine pronouns make the same point as her pseudonym: while George Eliot "shared in the characteristic pattern of stress experienced by the men of letters of her day,"[55] her stress was that of a woman writer with a professional vocation. So that if John Blackwood was doubtful about the scheme to publish *Romola* "in fragments" in *Maga,* intending "to have decided on the form of publication when I had read the M.S.,"[56] in the event that decision was not to be his. George Eliot was ready to go to Smith, Elder, where George Smith, dissuading the Leweses from publishing *Romola* as a "serial" (i.e., part-issue), was yet eager to publish it in *The Cornhill* in "considerable installments."[57] Clearly, publishing format had been a "point of difficulty" between Blackwoods and the Leweses, but the significance of the episode lies there, in the difficulty and its resolution, rather than in the possibility that the economic outcome suggests that John Blackwood had been somehow "right" in his plans for *Romola*. Blackwood's "unvarying policy of never making offers for works unseen"[58] is another symptom of the petty-commodity relations of production within which George Eliot's professional concerns were irrelevant; Lewes's rationalization for part-issue or serial publication, "the advantage to such a work of being read slowly and deliberately,"[59] is similarly symptomatic, from the other side, of how those concerns were mediated by the struggle over format. It is that terrain, the terrain of difficulty and struggle, that is implied by the history of *The Mill* and of *Romola*, for the professional George Eliot, concerned about her financial responsibilities "in the present" but driven, too, by "the grand anxiety of doing my work worthily," was finally also concerned

> to have freedom to write out one's own varying unfolding self, and not be a machine always grinding out the same material or spinning the same sort of web.[60]

The professional's freedom to control conditions, terms, and content is never so manifest as when "he does something else than what was expected of him."

The arrangement with Blackwoods for the publication of *Middlemarch*, read in the context of this developing professional project as a woman writer, can thus be seen to be far more than a set of "marketing decisions" to which is attributable "whatever integrity *Middlemarch* does have."[61] While the production of *Middlemarch* represents "an adjustment of reciprocal interests" between author and publisher, the author's interest in format went beyond a simple compromise between a four-volume novel, unacceptable to John Blackwood, and conventional magazine serialization or part-issue, unacceptable to George Eliot. What had to be renegotiated were the relations of production of her novels, relations of production which would constitute and acknowledge her professional status. George Eliot and Lewes, for instance, saw the proposed new format as reopening so basic a matter as who was to take the risk of publication, whether the publisher, who would then offer a cash sum of £6,000 for the four-year English copyright, or George Eliot, freely writing out her own varying unfolding self, taking the risk and a 40 percent royalty on her own success.[62] Such freedom was part and parcel of George Eliot's individual professional project; much more than merely an unlikely female entrepreneur, she arranges the production of *Middlemarch* to the form of her professional commitment as a writer, finally displaying publicly her own control not only over the terms, conditions, and content, but over the setting in which she performs her work. The compromise worked out, the final step in her individual professional project, is a compromise also between commodity-book and commodity-text. To the extent that she freely, riskily, and successfully interpellated a special audience outside of Mudie's, she had escaped the hegemonic structures of the market for commodity-books. To the extent, on the other hand, that she conformed to those market structures she was producing a commodity-book; W. H. Smith circulated the "Books" of *Middlemarch*, the bimonthly parts, as if they were volumes of a three-decker, the format encouraging the illusion until Lewes allowed publisher's advertisements, a hallmark of the monthly number, to be added at the back.[63] But George Eliot's project was to become a professional woman writer, not by revolutionizing the literary mode of production but by changing the social relations of her own production of novels.

Middlemarch may be seen, then, as a text determined in part by the historical project of professionalization: determined, that is, by the literary mode of production and by the relations of professionals to the forms of capitalist production, but determined also by the ideological exclusion of women from professions and by individualist, positivist ideology. The text of *Middlemarch* "traces" these multiple determinations in the presentment, for example, of its theme of "vocation"; the text generally subsumes "profession" under "vocation" and that is the site of a major contradiction. For to see professionalization historically as not at all "the idea of vocation in its industrial manifestation," but instead as a project of occupational organization for control of the relations of production and to the exclusion of women, is to recognize that Lydgate's "career" cannot be explained simply as being "set in the individualist phase of the modern medical profession,"[64] for historically professionalization never had an "individualist" phase. The individualism of critics' historical explanations, but also of Lydgate's fictional career, are determinate ideological effects; for example, Leavis's emphasis on her "profound analysis of the individual and its psychological dangers for George Eliot," and her "sheer informedness about society [and] the ways in which people of different classes . . . earn their livelihoods,"[65] by its own individualism and empiricism, makes it impossible to see those historical livelihoods as socially and ideologically constructed, or to see their relationship to *Middlemarch* as more than simple historical "background." A more precise historical explanation would see George Eliot's portrayal of Lydgate's attempt to earn a livelihood as a determinate ideological effect of the willed insertion of her woman's professional project into a profession of authorship which constructs women as amateurs.

For during the fusion of the original "Middlemarch" and "Miss Brooke" stories in 1870–71, George Eliot made substantial changes in content and thematic orientation, as she moved *Middlemarch* towards its varied enactment of "the mixed result of young and noble impulse struggling under prosaic conditions."[66] She discovered and defined the "much richer conception" of the theme which she was to set out in the "Prelude," displacing Fred Vincy's search for a vocation from its simple contrast with Lydgate's, and moving Lydgate to the fore as "the direct counterpart of Dorothea," as she changed Rosamond's character and her relation to Lydgate.[67] "What seems to have been, at first, an account of three parallel attempts to discover vocation," says Stanton Millett, now begins to emerge as a coherent study of interrelated characters, each demonstrating some measure of "high ideals" and "great resolve," each discovering that achievement is fundamentally conditioned by mundane details of "domestic reality."[68]

This matter of the fusion of the two early stories must be approached very gingerly; as Jerome Beaty points out, the similarities between the lives of Lydgate and Dorothea, so obvious to readers of the finished novel, should not be treated as the simple, sole reason for joining them. There were other similarities in the two stories, of time and geographical setting, and he argues that George Eliot was perhaps only "primed" to see them when she finished the first major plot line of "Miss Brooke," when on 31 December 1870, during her habitual year-end review of her accomplishments, she remembered "Middlemarch."[69] Moreover, the decision to join the two stories saddled her with the prospect of a novel of unconventional length and "too many momenti." These two aspects of her compositional problem she dealt with by devising with Lewes the new format, but also by rethinking the "momenti" of the original "Middlemarch." For whereas George Eliot did not find it necessary to rewrite or even to recopy "Miss Brooke," which became the first nine and a half chapters of the new novel, "*not one page* of the original draft of the earlier 'Middlemarch' remains,"[70] and it is in what she apparently did to "Middlemarch," "the medical novel,"[71] that we can begin to see the traces of the overdetermined relation between that project of composition, George Eliot's own project as a woman writer, and the historical project of professionalization. For if George Eliot is showing in Lydgate's story "the emergence of a new kind of doctor, with new status and new ideas of medical practice,"[72] the kind of doctor Lydgate was to be, and how the historical process of its "emergence" was to be presented, apparently changed from "Middlemarch" to *Middlemarch*. It is not simply the addition of "details of the status of medical practice and research" which must be noted, or that the thrust of her revisions throughout the manuscript was always toward adding new material and toward reorganization of what she had written, never toward cancellation of material or toward the simple replacement of one version by another.[73]

What took place, I am arguing, was not simple at all, but a complex rethinking of Lydgate as a professional, precipitated perhaps by "Miss Brooke" but determined by the constant pressure of George Eliot's own professional project.

Chapter 15, in which the reader is introduced to Lydgate's past, his medical education and ambitions, and his brief infatuation with Laure, would appear to be the remains of the original "introduction" to "Middlemarch." "Basic to the organization of this part of the novel," indeed even the "genetic center of the text," the chapter was once "many pages longer," and the account of Lydgate's background, "now available in a somewhat expanded form," was "heavily revised" and "reorganized."[74] And what Chapter 15 now does is to make a profession into a vocation:[75] Lydgate's "two purposes" are the "pursuit of a great idea" and "the assiduous practice of his profession" (1:261), with the emphasis placed on his "intellectual passion" (1:256), the "general advance" being but one aim of "his own scientific pursuits" (1:259). But amidst the details of Lydgate's commitment to "the independent value of his own work" there are two ironic references to another conception of "professionalism": the narrator refers to

venerable colleges which used great efforts to secure purity of knowledge by making it scarce, and to exclude error by a rigid exclusiveness in relation to fees and appointments (1:259),

and to

the high standard held up to the public mind by the College of Physicians, which gave its peculiar sanction to the expensive and highly-rarified medical instruction obtained by graduates of Oxford and Cambridge. (1:259)

The significance of these two references is precisely that they appear to lead nowhere in the finished novel; while the social status of various medical men is commented on ironically, the narrator never again refers to the very structures of professionalization, or justifies the heavy irony of these two passages. But in the notebooks which George Eliot kept for *Middlemarch* we find both the exploration of the structures of medicine's professional project in the early nineteenth century and the mordant irony. Amidst the information George Eliot collected on the history of medical prognosis and treatment and of contagion, on heart disease, cholera, typhus/typhoid, and *delerium tremens*, and on "the scientific method,"[76] there are also entries on the "folk concept" of medical professionalism, the distinctions made between the different kinds of practitioners, their training and status, and the lives of eminent scientific thinkers.[77] But what is particularly striking is the number and diversity of entries relating to professionalism in its strict historical sense, to the apparatuses of professionalization. For while she records the special qualifications of medical practitioners and their special kinds of knowledge, George Eliot also records how these were used to organize the occupation with an eye towards controlling the terms, conditions, and content of work, free of the authority of others, towards, finally, the monopolization of status and work privileges. Her "Quarry for Middlemarch," for example, records her interest in articles in the *Lancet* on "Willcocks' 'Laws relating to the Medical Prof.' " and on "Medical Polity." She notes the privileges ("exclusively of their own manufacture") of the College of Physicians, the privileges of apothecaries, and the sanctions taken on 10 December 1830 by the Derbyshire Medical and Surgical Society against a medical man who had undercharged in midwifery cases, "in gross violation of the rules of the profession."[78] She is interested in scales of fees in Manchester, nepotism in hospitals, and "the injurious effects of the monopoly by usurpation of the Royal Coll. of Phys. 1826," commenting at one point:

> Curious to observe, on the one hand, the College
> of Physicians procuring a law enabling them to
> prohibit surgeons from practising physic, & on
> the other, a law authorizing themselves to prac-
> tise surgery.

"Monopoly" is the perceived aim not only of the College of Physicians but of the graduates of Oxford and Cambridge, yet the College of Surgeons was "just as restrictive"; she comments on a decree that only certain schools of surgery would be recognized: "This of course repressed the salutary competition of private with endowed teachers."[79] In another notebook she records a narrative summary, taken from other sources, of the professionalization of apothecaries, which she entitles "Medical Profession."[80]

None of this, of course, engages Lydgate's career, nor anything else, except for the two passages I have mentioned, in the text of *Middlemarch*. Lydgate's commitment to "the independent value of his own work" (1:132) has no relation whatever to "the high standard held up to the public mind by the College of Physicians"; the possibility of an ironical contrast is never developed. The understanding evinced in the notebooks of professionalization as the exclusionary organization of a whole occupation is merely "traced" in those references. Indeed, the narrative's free indirect discourse often serves to ensure that the only understanding of medicine as an emerging profession is that of the partisan practitioners in Middlemarch. Wrench and Toller, who have long-established Middlemarch practices, consider Lydgate a "jackanapes" for not dispensing drugs himself. Their judgment of Lydgate is presented in free indirect discourse:

> It was clear that Lydgate . . . intended to cast imputations on his equals, and also to obscure the limit between his own rank as a general practitioner and that of the physicians, who, in the interest of the profession, felt bound to maintain its various grades (1:329).

The narrative here limits our perception of "the profession" to that of either insiders who benefit individually from its limits, ranks, and grades, or those who would oppose them "professionally." As we have seen, this is a version of the "folk concept" of profession. For if free indirect discourse is "an utterance where two voices, that of the character and that of the narrator, co-exist in a structure of undecidability," presenting a "double view,"[81] here the un-decidability also indicates a decision not to see profession historically. The irony which may interrupt the free indirect discourse never, except in those traced passages, disturbs the text's discourse, in the broader sense, of the folk concept of profession; Lydgate "had not been to either of the English universities and enjoyed the absence of anatomical and bedside study there" (1:329), but so to comment is not to acknowledge the structuring of exclusive privilege and the repression of salutary competition which George Eliot had mentioned in the notebooks. And the text of *Middlemarch* nowhere acknowledges these; the profession of medicine is treated throughout on the level of "vocation," individual-ized to such an extent that the novel, neither in its ironies nor elsewhere, implies a judgment on the characteristics of medicine as an evolving profession more historically com-prehending than Wrench's concern for "etiquette" (3:39)— sociologically "an expression of occupational solidarity"—[82] or Lydgate's personal program: "A change in the units was the most direct mode of changing the numbers" (1:260).

For that reductive, personalized, individual level is the very level on which the text can make these concerns avail-able, as metaphor, for the vocations of the other main char-acters, most particularly Dorothea, whose exclusion from more strictly professional aspirations we experience but cannot question historically.[83] The reorganization of "Mid-dlemarch," I am arguing, was in part a redefining of Lyd-gate's professional life, redirected towards his vocational commitment, while as part of the same process Dorothea's woman's search for a vocation was brought forward, a point of similarity having been found. The determinate indi-vidualism of George Eliot's own professional project— "building my own house" within ideological structures of authorship which try to locate her as an "amateur," as "au-thoress"—thus determines through Dorothea the indi-vidualist nature of Lydgate's professional project. "George Eliot," the pseudonym, signifies the historical specifics of that determinate process, the insertion, that is, of the ideo-logically structured situation of a particular Victorian woman writer into the social, economic, and ideological structures of book production in 1870. The result of this whole process is indeed a compromise, one which is the product of George Eliot's individual struggle within the relations of novel production, a text which, while interpellating her own readers by writing out her own varying, unfolding, professional self, assumes with its format and the stately pace of the book's distribution the dignity and grandeur of the Blackwood-Mudie three-decker. Barbara Hardy has noticed in *Middlemarch*, George Eliot's "most feminist novel," an insistence on "undifferentiated humanity, on man and woman."[84] The text had been rethought, not only so as to allow a female character an "equivalent centre of self" (1:382) to (among others) a male professional, but so to present "profession" as to ignore those historical features which would deny and prevent equivalency. As a successful commodity-text, *Middlemarch* interpellates that "feminist" reader who, like George Eliot, saw the married women's property petition as "one round of a long ladder stretching far beyond our lives."[85] That ideological position, that particular "feminism" or, more generally, "meliorism" or "contemplative materialism,"[86] was produced within the complex unity of George Eliot's situation as a woman writer, and within the forms which patriarchy took in publishing in England in 1870.

Four

Lateral Advance: *Tess* and the Necessities of Magazine Publication

In an essay on copyright, first published in the *Fortnightly Review* in March 1880, Matthew Arnold spoke of a "new *modus vivendi* in literature."[1] Arnold had borrowed the phrase from George Sand, and its immediate reference was to the "industrial and literary revolution" in France which, he writes, "may be summed up in two words: *'cheap books'*" (114). Arnold is himself concerned about the situation in England. His point of departure was the Report and Minutes of the Royal Commission on Copyright which sat from 1876 to 1878, and the particular value of his essay derives from the way in which he characteristically attempts to comment from "neither an author's point of view, nor a publisher's point of view, nor yet the point of view of one contending against authors and publishers, but the point of view of one whose sole wish is to let things appear . . . as they really are" (117). From that interesting position Arnold attempts to broaden the discussion from "the proprietary right of the author" (117) and international copyright to what might be the possibility and the implications of the new *modus vivendi* for English publishing.

He is impatient with the commissioners' conclusion in 1878 that copyright should continue to be treated as a proprietary right, believing that "this metaphysical phantom of property in itself . . . like other metaphysical phantoms, is hollow and leads us to delusion." Property does not exist "in itself," Arnold writes,

> Property is the creation of law. It is effect given, by society and its laws, to that natural instinct in man which makes him seek to enjoy ownership in what he produces, acquires or has. (120)

Typically, Matthew Arnold has much to say about "the instinct of ownership" (120), as well as, yet again, "the instinct of expansion, the instinct of self-preservation" (116), but his primary focus on "society and its laws" allows him momentarily to escape idealist moralizing and to comment on "the highly unsatisfactory system of our book trade" (126). For Arnold recognizes that at that time in England the author's "instinct for ownership" was sharply contradicted by "a general impatience at the dearness of new books" (123); "the three-shilling book is our great want" (126), he says, and yet it is denied by "the system which keeps up the present exorbitant price of new books in England, the system of lending-libraries from which books are hired," which is "eccentric, artificial, and unsatisfactory in the highest degree" (125). Arnold's essay, for all his need again to trundle forward "sweetness and light," Grub Street (131), and those various "instincts," nevertheless to some degree historicizes the 1870s debate on copyright in useful, materialist terms. Indeed, the context to which he points makes it clear that the issue, even if it is seen as "author's rights" or "the price of books," is not an issue merely of the 1870s at all. Rather it had its origins in the construction of "our system," the "procrustean bed" (as it was always called) of the dominant literary mode of production which was being awkwardly if inexorably transformed by economic, social, and ideological forces which had been operating for decades. The discussion of copyright, including Arnold's essay, or the discussion in the 80s of the "new journalism" (in which Arnold was to engage in another essay)[2] are merely symptoms of these processes, alluding to them obliquely by silence or oversight.

The development of the periodical press, newspapers and magazines, from the 1840s is perhaps the process in which the transformation of the mode of production registers itself most clearly in the actual social formation. The discussion of copyright after the Act of 1842, aside from the debate over international copyright, was to a large extent concerned with the act's not having considered specifically newspaper and magazine copyright. In the 1870s the Royal Commission attempted (amidst similar specifications about copyright in lectures, abridgements, encyclopedias, translations, and so on) to establish for periodicals the forms of contractural agreement which would define authors' and proprietors' rights, not only to original copyright but to separate publication, as well as specifying whose responsibility it was to prevent piracy.[3] The subsequent court cases over whether a newspaper or magazine was a book, and then over how the separate articles making it up were to be registered for copyright,[4] mark the stages in an extended struggle between writers and publishers as new relations of production were set in place. The ambiguous silence regarding periodicals in the Act of 1842 had merely exposed the terrain for a struggle which, while settled in law by Dicks v. Yates (18 Ch. D. 76) in 1881, was still rumbling in the journals in the 1890s.[5] What was being fought over was again not only control of the product, of the book, but also control of the labor process and of the surplus value produced in the new, fully capitalist mode of production of the modern magazine or newspaper.

Seeing this whole historical process again dialectically, as the structuration of a new literary mode of production, we are able to escape generalizations about "this most characteristic manifestation of the exuberance of Victorian life—its periodical press,"[6] or the more whiggish empiricist statements about the "journalistic expansion during the Victorian period," cataloging the historical "benchmarks" such as "increased literacy, technological innovation, . . . a dramatic decline in the price of paper, more efficient distribution of copy, the removal of financial restraints."[7] While that is perhaps a useful list, it is merely a list of very disparate elements whose significance lies only in their relations to each other (and to others unlisted) on the economic and social levels of the Victorian social formation. Another kind

of partial genei alization derives the distinctiveness of Victorian periodical publication from changes on the ideological
level, usually pointing to some sort of watershed: by the
1890s assumptions were otherwise, but "in 1860, 1870 and
1880 it was still assumed that the papers were taken by
earnest-minded seekers after news to whom search was part
of the discipline which they readily exacted from
themselves."[8] Another newspaper history speaks of the
changing understanding, not of the readers but of the publishers in the period 1855–1914; there occurred

> a struggle between two conceptions of the press:
> the one of a Fourth Estate, with proprietorship a
> form of public service and journalists a species of
> public philosopher; the other of the press as an
> industry, with proprietors as businessmen and
> journalism as a trade or craft.[9]

And Fox Bourne, in his classic history of English newspapers, places the change historically in relation to the removal at mid-century of the "taxes on knowledge": "a great
cleavage began," he wrote, "or was then first apparent,
about the middle of the nineteenth century, and it was very
distinct before the day when the paper duty was done away
with."[10] Yet this ideological cleavage, or struggle, or change
of assumptions, must also be seen in relation to the struggle
over periodical copyright, to the technological changes and
the other "benchmarks" in the evolving literary mode of
production, and it is the articulation of those relations which
must be explained.

For in examining periodical publication in these decades
I do not mean to narrow my focus; I am arguing that "the
rise of the modern newspaper" is the most comprehensive
empirical description of the whole process, it it is constantly
seen as broadly overdetermined. One important determination was indeed what Alan Lee has called "those ex-
traordinary machines." I don't need to add to the many
accounts, Lee's and others',[11] of the invention of Applegath's vertical rotary-action press (1846), the Hoe horizon-
tal press (1846), and the Walter reel-fed rotary press (1868),
of stereotyping and of Hattersley's composing machine in

the 1850s. A. E. Musson, for example, has demonstrated in detail how the *Manchester Guardian*, by 1895, had undergone "an 'industrial revolution' in both press and composing departments." Musson's analysis is especially useful because his insistence on how little this mechanization resulted in worsening labor conditions raises precisely the issue of the social relations which accompanied the new means of production. The effects he records, the new distinctions introduced between workers, the employment of un-apprenticed youths, the institution of a set of bonus payments in the composing room, all point to the introduction of these machines not simply as resulting in "more, cheaper, and larger newspapers, with extra editions and supplements," but as the occasion of an intense struggle between proprietors and workers, as indicating in publishing the steady appropriation of labor-power as fixed capital.[12] These are not simply moments in a steady progress towards high-speed, "modern" production but manifestations of the same process in the struggle of capitalist enterprise towards the maximal appropriation of surplus value which had occurred in textile and other manufactures. The technological development in printing was but part of the whole transformation of a relatively autonomous sector in a complexly overdetermined historical process. Clearly it contributed, with the abolition of the "taxes on knowledge," to the "lowering of the cost of production" of which Fox Bourne speaks.[13] But the lowered costs of production were in no way a sufficient cause of the transformation in the production of periodicals; as Howe points out,

> Newspaper proprietors could afford to experiment with new and expensive plant, because the time was to come, probably after 1860, when the cost of printing a newspaper and the revenue from sales bore no relationship to the greatly superior income and profit from the sale of advertising space.[14]

To emphasize, then, or even merely to take at face value the impact of the new machines on the production of periodicals, and then to see the lower-priced newspaper successfully competing solely for that reason, would be grossly to oversimplify the historical change. The Stamp Acts, for example, had necessarily put a premium on space on a newspaper page and had forced the tight-packing of the dailies, characteristically the *Times*. But the removal of duties did not mean that papers could easily change to a less black page. The "traditionalist, pack-it-in, single-column approach"[15] was bound up in ideology; it had become an "upper- and middle-class typographical orthodoxy," taking its aura of "quality" from the *Times*, so that the typography of the new press of the 1850s ran the risk of being perceived as "cheap."[16] And the same dialectical complexity operated on other levels: another instance of the complexity of the historical dynamics is the way that the telegraph and railways, while contributing to the expansion and centralization of the London press,[17] yet enabled the striking growth of a weekly, and even a daily, provincial press, by the distribution, for example, to provincial printers of Charles Knight's partially printed sheets from London.[18] And on yet another level, "the changing status of the journalist" after the 1840s was produced by their struggle, as the forces and relations of production also changed around them.[19]

The transformation in the production of novels during these years has also often been viewed in oversimplified ways, the flourishing of the serial in weekly or monthly periodicals being seen similarly as a matter of changed technology, of lowering the costs of production and competing on the level of price. We may doubt Matthew Arnold's belief that "there is a need for cheaper books" because, as he believes, "the victory will be with good books in the end,"[20] but we might question as well Kathleen Tillotson's only less moralized free-market assumptions about the history of serial novel publication: "in the end one form of cheap publication devoured the other: the part-issue was driven off the market by its rival the magazine serial."[21] Graham Pollard's version of the same argument is more guarded; the establishment of the shilling magazine, he writes, simply "reacted on the popularity of the part issue," but he also quickly implies a new kind of production process: "serialization possessed the advantage over part issue in that it capitalized the goodwill of successful novel."[22] For the development of fiction-carrying periodicals, from the 1850s on, was "part of the logic of the increasing growth and power of a nucleus of very large firms,"[23] and more basically, I am arguing, part of the logic of development of capitalist novel production itself. The interplay between the contrasting possibilities inherent in part-issue production on the one hand and, on the other, the dominant, "eccentric" lending-library system indicates just how. The hegemonic system, based on a high initial price for a three-volume novel, generated, as we have seen, large profits which were divided among publisher, library, and author. But the very safety of this mode of petty-commodity book production precluded its achieving the profits attainable by the capitalist production, in part-issue, of commodity-texts. The surplus value of the commodity-text was made possible by capitalist control, to a greater extent, of the actual production process, a form of alienation which the writer, to some extent, might resist, as Dickens occasionally did successfully, as in the process of producing *Pickwick Papers*. To that extent, part-issue was, for the capitalist publisher, an imperfect form of commodity-text production; control of the production process was erratic, the process itself being potentially a disruptive moment of class struggle. The structures of magazine serial publication, on the other hand, allowed a far more subtle and effective form of control of the production of commodity-texts. Control of the product, i.e. copyright in the text, might be negotiated in advance, but control of the actual production of a serial for a magazine or weekly newspaper did not need to be negotiated; it was a *given*. The writer's work was produced in a journal within relations of production analogous to those prevailing in a textile mill. When the *Bolton Weekly Journal*, for example, announced itself as "Liberal," and as "probably the English newspaper distinctively wedded to the publication of fiction, as a feature of the family newspaper," and then went on to extol its "Ladies Column, Children's Hour, London Letter, and other special articles," or when the *Graphic*, to take another instance, advertised itself as "Independent. An admirably illustrated journal, combining 'Literary excellence with artistic beauty,'"[24] fiction writers entered their pages as hand-loom weavers entered a factory, knowing that within that space the publisher had a wide choice of methods with which to capitalize "the goodwill of a novel." These were what Thomas Hardy was to experience as "the necessities of magazine publication,"[25] and it is the specific forms of those "necessities" which must be analyzed historically.

The main forms of capitalist control of serial novel production in magazines at mid-century were the new division of periodicals into "clique" or "class"[26] journals, and the growing use of wood-block illustration. While each of these has its own independent causality, historically they come together with certain ideological determinants to constitute the "new journalism" of the 1880s and 90s. I shall return to the "new journalism," but here I want to consider how a "class" journal—"a periodical . . . designed to meet the interests of a definable group of potential subscribers"[27]— represented a form of control, while permitting (*by* permitting) the particular kinds of interpellation which were to characterize the "new journalism." Charles Morgan was to regret the passing of the "liberal tradition" in magazines, of such "civilized" journals as *Macmillan's*—"We have specialized in this as in all else"[28]—and Fox Bourne discussed several sorts of specialized, "miscellaneous" class and clique journalism, beginning with the pictorial journalism inaugurated in 1842 by the *Illustrated London News*.[29] Walter Besant reminded young writers in 1899 that "every journal has its own *clientèle*,"[30] and it is important to recognize how that new kind of readership was constituted and how it functioned. For the "class" journal did not address social groupings as it found them, always/already given (a *class*, for instance), but rather reconstituted their members into a specialized clientele, "extremely diversified"[31] perhaps, but an audience with "a market character,"[32] consuming a new kind of "branded goods."[33] This was the new "shrill capitalized format" within which the "intellectually more passive, morally less confident reader" was appealed to, indeed by which that reading subject was constructed, establishing a set of "reading relations," in Tony Bennett's phrase, or "social relations of reading," for the "superintendence of popular reading."[34] As Oscar Maurer put it many years ago, "here we are plainly approaching the realm of pre-tested consumer response, if not of the engineering of consent,"[35] and the manipulation which he describes is directly connected to the new kinds of control over production of the written text through the formal requirements of the new "class" journalism.

That magazine illustration, too, was a means of managerial control of the production of a text again is obscured by the complex detail of its own specific history. There was little question, says Alan Lee, that the increased use of illustration from the 1840s "served to broaden the horizons of its audience and to reduce parochialism";[36] the specific forms which "broadening" and "reducing" might take will be discussed later, while I glance here at the historical transformations which produced those processes while obscuring or mystifying them. For this production of magazines was "a crucial element in the economic structure that made illustration attractive to artists and engravers alike."[37] The *Illustrated London News* was started, and large blocks and quick engraving came to be in demand, "just about the time" that engraved wood blocks were adapted to the new presses, being bolted together to print large plates.[38] The illustrated newspaper, Mason Jackson asserted, "owes its existence" to the art of wood-engraving, and in describing the process of preparing a sketch for a half-page block, he stresses also the necessary further process of "subduing" faulty or objectionable parts of the sketch without "doing violence to the general truth of the representation." His account makes clear the priorities and the degree of editorial control:

> Occasionally, when there is very great hurry, the block is separated piece by piece as fast as parts of the drawing are finished—the engraver and draughtsman thus working on the same subject at the same time. Instances have occurred where the draughtsman had done his work in this way, and has never seen the whole of his drawing together.[39]

Another historian, remarking that the discovery in the 60s of a method of photographing drawings on wood "intro-

duced an entirely new mechanical element into the reproduction process," concluded that this "destroyed the vital
link between the artist and the finished product," so that
finally "the engraver was susperseded."[40] Within such relations of production it might well be "held essential that some
one with a strong artistic faculty should be constantly on the
watch, as a protection against the carelessness or forgetful-
ness of the artist, and, it may be, to suggest alterations in his
drawings."[41] Like the restructuring of "class" journalism,
the new practices of magazine illustration represent the
constitution of the new forms of control of the production
of texts necessary to the fully capitalist "new journalism."

But "the development of class magazines as a commercial
enterprise," the "new journalism" of the 1850s and 60s,[42]
was simply a moment, like the development of new techniques of illustration, in the whole process culminating in
the "new journalism" of the 1880s and 90s. That later enterprise can best be seen as consolidating the ideological practices of the new capitalist mode of literary production, the
production of commodity-texts in illustrated periodicals for
the widest possible audience of a specific, predetermined
"class." It was at once "a mixture of journalistic and typographical devices" and the new market, or "class," ideology I
have described, moving towards the concept of "branded
goods" developed, as we shall see, at the turn of the century.
As one historian writes:

> The "new journalism" of the 1880s . . . recog-
> nized that journalism took place within an ever-
> burgeoning market. The interests of the reader
> were an unplumbed well which could be ex-
> plored and re-explored forever. Journalism be-
> came the art of structuring reality, rather than
> recording it. . . . The journalist looks—
> metaphorically speaking—now to his right, now
> to his left, as he searches for the senses in which
> his account will be accepted within the rubric of
> objectivity. In performing this very task, he
> weaves the tapestry of reality which society
> accepts—or rejects—as being a true image of
> "things as they really are." The journalist has

come to supply the needs of a large social machinery which defines the interim phases of reality. The techniques of journalism have come to consist in skilful filling of pre-defined genres, each of which stands for a certain definition of the audience's needs.[43]

What needs here to be emphasized is that the writer's task in defining reality, "within the rubric of objectivity," was itself being thus newly defined, a writer's place in the social apparatus newly determined, and skill reduced or restricted to the filling of predefined genres, even to a certain predefined style.

The style of this new ideology of production was characterized, first of all, by brevity and personality. Newspaper histories emphasize how the news, for example, was to be "parcelled up into short and easily digestable portions,"[44] what Charles Morgan was to dismiss as "little buzzing attempts to suprise and titillate."[45] T. P. O'Connor of the *Star*, however, explained that although perhaps there might be in the "new journalism," as in a street piano, "a certain absence of soul," the notes should come out "clear, crisp, sharp." Like Macaulay's prose style, the "new journalism" was more interesting precisely because of "the infinitude of its petty details."[46] The other, related, stylistic feature of the new journalistic practices was "personality," as epitomized in the personal interview, that "impertinent practice of intruding on public men."[47] Denounced as an "outrage upon the private life of an individual," the interview embodied the "more personal tone" which O'Connor saw as a main point of difference between the "new" and the old. He himself applauded a practice so much in accord with that of Macaulay and Carlyle, as leading to understanding and appreciation of the character of public men: "What lends effect to the speeches of Mr. Parnell? . . . It is mainly the strong personality that one sees behind the words."[48] But, concentrating in this way on what came to be called "human interest," the "new journalism" limited itself to the "temporary and emotional effect," the emphasis on "personality," emotion and the spurious "experiential" immediacy of the interview, inviting only "a quick understanding of the smaller emotions,"[49] and presenting that as "natural" and inevitable.

The ideology of production, in the forms which I have been describing, thus necessarily controlled (or determined) the ways in which a journal interpellated its particular readership, its "clientele," and the *Graphic* in the late 1880s and 90s shows clearly in its format the forces and relations we have been describing and their ideologies. The issue for 18 July 1891,[50] for example, surrounded the first installment of *Tess of the D'Urbervilles* with five full-page prints of episodes connected with the visit of the German emperor, including two double-page prints of the emperor reviewing the volunteers at Wimbledon (this had occurred only seven days earlier, and so was commemorated with very great speed). The two-page commentary on the events recorded from the imperial visit presumably substituted for the *Graphic's* usual column explaining "Our Illustrations," which along with such other regular columns as "Topics of the Week," "Pastimes" (sports), "Home," "Foreign," "The Court," and "Rural Notes," indicate the principles of organization, the kinds of understanding assumed by the *Graphic* and its "class." In the issue for 28 November, to take another example, the news is characteristically "personal": "Topics of the Week" include paragraphs on "Lord Salisbury at Birmingham," "The French Miners' Appeal" (to British miners for strike funds), the death of Bulwer-Lytton, and the problems the "modern British soldier" was supposed to be having with his boots. The "personality" and brevity mark the topics so arbitrarily selected as "news," as they mark the comments on new novels and foreign affairs; these events of contemporary life are selected and reduced, constituted not only as topics but as facts by their brief acknowledgment in the pages of the *Graphic*. And it is this very process of structuration which controls the production of *Tess of the D'Urbervilles* as a commodity-text. For we are speaking here of the text of *Tess* as the determinate effect of a series of determinate acts of production. As Tony Bennett has pointed out, "the text which readers encounter is already 'over-worked,' 'over-coded,' productively activated in a particular way as a result of its inscription within the social, material, ideological and institutional relationships which distinguish specific reading relations."[51] Historically, those relationships were inscribed in *Tess* by its publication in the *Graphic*, in the midst of the "class" interests I have mentioned, but more particularly by the kinds of illustrations and revisions enforced by the *Graphic*'s "class" of journal. The *Graphic* as a whole, as we shall see from three specific examples of the production of *Tess* as a commodity-text, was an apparatus of ideological control: in order to be published there ("for the privilege of writing in the English language"),[52] Hardy's manuscript text was submitted to the forms of control we have outlined, to the determinations of "class" embodied in the surrounding contents of the *Graphic*, to the determinations of a process of illustration controlled by "someone with a strong artistic faculty," and to the ideological determinations of the format and style of the "new journalism." The resulting product is *Tess* as a commodity-text, interpellating its reader as the *Graphic*'s "class" subject.

That subject is interpellated in complex ways; if, for instance, "Hardy's watching presence," or at least that of his narrator, "is the most fundamental stability in the novel,"[53] that presence was produced in the *Graphic* so as necessarily to interpellate its "class" subject. Discussing Hardy's narrative mode generally, Hillis Miller notes how Hardy is "adept at making small shifts in perspective":

> The reader is made aware that there are two ways
> of seeing events, a way which takes what is seen as
> the whole span of reality, and one which sees any
> perspective as only one among many possibilities
> and therefore as relative in the value it gives to
> things.[54]

Terry Eagleton makes a similar but more specific comment on narrative perspective, remarking that the farm-laborers in *Tess* are seen in two different lights, one "natural," one "transformative," living "within this acute contradiction between a sense of themselves as uniquely individual, and that sense of themselves mediated to them by an observer's vantage point,"[55] and he then alludes to the episode in *Tess* in which Farmer Crick and his farmer laborers search the dry-mead for the garlic plant which had tainted the morning's milk:

> With eyes fixed upon the ground, they crept slowly across a strip of the field, returning a little further down in such a manner that, when they should have finished, not a single inch of the pasture but would have fallen under the eye of some one of them. . . .
> Differing one from another in natures and moods so greatly as they did, they yet formed a curiously-uniform row—automatic, noiseless; and an alien observer passing down the neighboring lane might well have been excused for massing them as "Hodge." (246)

As Eagleton points out, the text here makes a very careful statement about the farm workers' differences and yet their curious uniformity, excusing while clearly rejecting the "alien" tendency to reduce this complexity to the stereotype. But this episode was the one which the *Graphic* chose to be illustrated for its issue of 29 August. Significantly, the caption is Farmer Crick's exclamation when "straightening himself slowly with an excruciated look till quite upright" (245): "This here stooping do fairly make my back open and shut." In the written text Crick's exclamation simply explains his withdrawal from the search, which in turn allows Tess and Angel to drop behind and talk privately. But the "tableau" which the illustration presents, with its "visually pleasing" major diagonal line of figures, is indeed "an effective pastoral scene"[56] of a certain type, as it literally foregrounds the be-smocked Crick as "Hodge," speaking his quaintly rustic piece to that alien observer, the reader of the *Graphic*. Hardy's written text has been reproduced pictorially as commodity-text, itself reproducing the "class" ideology of the *Graphic*. That same issue of the *Graphic* also contains, as its other "pastoral" content, items on "Farmers and Trespassers" (238) and on the effects of rainfall on the year's harvest (253), and a brief review of a book extolling the fine prospects in Australia or New Zealand for "a hard-working young farmer with a capital of 1,000£" (255).

These tidbits (for they are all very brief) might be said, despite their summariness, to "structure reality," to "define the interim phases of reality," locating the reader of the *Graphic* as a "class" subject. Farmer Crick as rustic interpellates that same "class" subject, an alien observer to Hardy's written text, but the correct consumer of the commodity-text. The *Graphic* as a "class" ideological apparatus necessarily assumes such stereotypes. Its format, made up of "facts," tidbits and personalities, precludes the challenging or testing of "class" generalizations; they are always/already assumed, in both senses. *Tess of the D'Urbervilles*, appearing in the *Graphic*, can only become a commodity-text, "tracing" its mode of production by interpellating the reader as an appropriate "class" subject. In another example of how the illustrations control the ideological vantage point, the two-page illustration of the first installment on 4 July (12-13), pictures Tess returning home from the "club-walking" or May Day dance. Arlene Jackson comments that "the scene in the textual presentation is not particularly dramatic," and she goes on to applaud the "dramatic impact" of the engraving, its "dramatic handling of large blocks of light and dark tones."[57] The written text is indeed not dramatic: the narrative vantage point is deep in Tess's "anxious" consciousness. As she opens the door to her parents' cottage, "the interior . . . struck upon the girl's senses with an unspeakable dreariness," and Tess feels "the jar of contrast" and a "chill feeling of self-reproach" (14). The *Graphic*'s illustration, however, shifts the vantage point from Tess entirely; the caption, following the text, announces, "there stood her mother, amid the group of children, hanging over the washing-tub," and there indeed they are, while the viewer is placed well behind the mother and children, facing Tess, who is radiant in her white dress (a "large block of light tones"), framed by the doorway, the focus of all eyes but those of the baby in the cradle, whose direct gaze at the reader fixes the changed vantage point. The *Graphic*'s engraving, while perhaps enforcing what Arlene Jackson calls "the domestic theme conveyed through the illustrations as a series," thus also personalizes the scene around Tess, her dress, her expression, even her posture, and by so dramatizing "young maiden innocence"[58] (with which the written text is not at this moment concerned) again bends the text to its ideological purpose, interpellating the reader as the *Graphic*'s "class" subject. The purpose of magazines like the *Graphic*, writes Hardy in 1890, "is not upward advance but lateral advance; to suit themselves to what is called household reading."[59] The *Graphic* might be said here to have shifted Hardy's vantage point "laterally," by its illustration, to precisely that end.

A more complex example of the *Graphic*'s "superintendence" of the text of *Tess of the D'Urbervilles* occurs with the episode in Angel and Tess's courtship, illustrated on 26 September (357), in which, one morning after Tess had awakened Angel and the other dairy workers, the lovers meet on the stairway of the sleeping quarters. The control exerted here by the conditions of publication in the *Graphic* is more complex in that it extends not only to the effects of the illustration but to textual emendation (or "censorship") and even to punctuation. The caption to the illustration is "Clare came down from the landing above in his shirtsleeves and put his arm across the stairway." In the written text Angel addresses Tess as "Miss Flirt" and asks her to respond finally to his marriage proposal. What appear to be the main ideological issues to be settled for the commodity-text are the degree of inwardness, and especially sexuality, to be allowed Tess, and the degree of Angel's sexual excitement at this moment. The illustration, in its caption, changes the written text's "he" to "Clare," thus fixing the male figure not as "Angel" and certainly not as the object of Tess's intimate consciousness, which is the vantage point in Hardy's description of the encounter. Indeed the illustration presents not Tess's perspective on Angel at all but rather a view of Tess by candlelight at the top of the stairs, from a vantage point behind Angel's back. The *Graphic* text, as does the manuscript,[60] describes him as "in his shirtsleeves, without any shoes" (358), but the illustration shows Angel's legs only to the calf. Thus the illustration has bent the scene to particular social conventions by its arrangement and focus, presenting Tess, as these illustrations so often do (101, 133,

217, 273, 670-71), not as the conscious agent in a complexly determined moment but as a woman who has been accosted while alone, who yet is protected by rules of decorum, asserted here "pictorially." This decorum, so necessary to the commodity-text, was asserted in other ways as well in the "dual process of adaptation and revision" of the episode which, J. T. Laird has shown, emerged "out of both freedom and necessity."[61] The sentence in the *Graphic* version in which Tess "tried to smile away the seriousness of her words" may have been merely a compositor's mistake for "the seriousness of his words,"[62] but the same effect of reducing Tess's sexual independence is achieved by the *Graphic*'s suppression of her "pout" when she asks him not to call her "Flirt."[63] Furthermore, Simon Gatrell, in his Editorial Introduction to *Tess* and elsewhere, makes a convincing case for the effect of the *Graphic*'s punctuation practice in shaping the text. While he suggests that there was so little agreement among the *Graphic*'s compositors that "the notion of a consistently viewed and imposed house-style begins to melt,"[64] nevertheless there are generalizations to be made from what the *Graphic* did to Hardy's punctuation. The text of the *Graphic*, Gatrell says, was set up "for the eye alone, so that the contemporary reader should find his grammatical expectations fulfilled,"[65] and I would add that what was contemporary about those expectations was determined by the "new journalism." The "salient feature" of the imposed punctuation was "uniformity," effectively reducing the "flow of excited talk" in Hardy's manuscript to "the speech of people who are thinking about what they are saying."[66] The encounter of Tess and Angel on the stairs is a case in point, the "uniform" punctuation in the *Graphic* reinforcing the textual decorum established by the illustration and the verbal revisions. The effect is precisely to impede the flow of excited talk, to isolate syntactically the units and qualities of the actions in the episode, as when the *Graphic* separates "he said" from "peremptorily" by a comma, instead of allowing Angel a degree of impetuosity. When Tess succumbs to Angel's insistence that she speak as a lover, the *Graphic* renders her submission thus: " 'Very well, then, Angel, dearest, if I *must*,' she said, looking at her candle," instead of the manuscript's "Very well, then: Angel dearest."[67] Here, it seems to me, the *Graphic* version clearly sacrifices the complex expression of one who asserts her self-control while yet submitting in a rush, a complexity of behavior which the practices of the *Graphic* and the "grammatical expectations of the contemporary reader" will not allow, to the speech of a person thinking primly and shallowly about what she is saying. The heavy punctuation here is thus a sign of complicity, of the "superintendence" in the production of *Tess* in the *Graphic*, "fixing the ideological co-ordinates within which the text is to be read."[68]

Not since Hardy's Explanatory Note to the First Edition of *Tess of the D'Urbervilles* in 1891 has it been possible to imagine that the *Graphic* was simply the innocent vehicle of the text of Hardy's novel. Indeed, since his acknowledgment there of the separate publication in the *Fortnightly* of "A Midnight Baptism," and of "Saturday Night in Arcady" in the *National Observer*,[69] much careful scholarship has clarified not only how Hardy proceeded to piece the novel together and print it complete, but also the history of its original composition. For these processes of composition, and then of "adaptation and revision," make up the project, from 1889 to 1891, of producing the commodity-text demanded by the *Graphic* and necessitated by a capitalist literary mode of production. Hardy's phrase, "this unceremonious concession to conventionality,"[70] too nervously compresses a production process determined by the forces and relations of magazine production, by the ideologies of "class" journalism and, by the late 80s, of the "new journalism." These constituted a fully capitalist mode of literary production, of which the "anticipatory censorship of editors and publishers" was but the most explicit manifestation. Hardy's own bitterness, Michael Millgate has suggested, was provoked by "his dismay at discovering that the editorial barriers at which he had directed his efforts were not in fact the ultimate strongholds of Grundyism but only its outworks."[71] I am further suggesting that "Grundyism" was itself but an ideological outwork; the "stronghold," or rather the determining structure, was the capitalist mode of production. Hardy's remark in "Candour in English Fiction," about "the fearful price" which the writer must pay "for the privilege of writing in the English language," dramatizes not merely his subjection to the Grundyist or to "conventionality" but also his relation to editor and publisher, compositor and illustrator. He complained in *The Early Life* that the labor of revising and adapting *Tess* for the *Graphic* "brought no profit."[72] It brought Thomas Hardy no profit, but for £550 and the privilege of writing in the English language he contributed to the production of the *Graphic*'s commodity-text, the serial *Tess of the D'Urbervilles*. The *Graphic*, "advancing laterally," did indeed make a profit, as its mode of production, in this very way, determined it should: it forced and shaped the "sheer drudgery" of Hardy's revisions, surrounded his text with illustrations, tidbits and advertisements so as to interpellate its "class" reader. And in that way, by those techniques, it "capitalized" to its own profit, in Graham Pollard's phrase, "the goodwill of a successful novel."

Five

Anyone of Everybody: Net Books and *Howards End*

In her book on Mudie's Library, Guinevere Griest's answer to her own question, "Who killed the three-decker?" is neither precise nor satisfying. She rightly dismisses the proud claims of individuals, of George Moore or his publisher, Henry Vizetelly, or of other publishers who had independently issued single-volume novels in the 1890s, but she then cites only "years of economic pressure" before shifting her attention completely: "What is remarkable about the end of the three-volume form is the completeness and rapidity of its disappearance."[1] Royal Gettmann, in the other extended study of the sudden disappearance of novels in the three-volume format, is more specific in assigning a cause—"the three-decker was bound to disappear because it had ceased to be profitable to the libraries"[2]—but he then becomes too engrossed in the "pounds, shillings and pence" of Mudie's diminishing profits (257-58). Gettmann's analysis is based on the account books and correspondence of the house of Bentley, so that his explanations tend often to elaborate Bentley's own, or those given in the letters from Mudie. At the end of the chapter on the three-decker he does allude to wider circumstances, to "confusion and uncertainty," "bewilderment and paralysis" in publishing, remarking ambiguously that the abolition of the old form meant, in effect, that "the publisher for the moment could not call the tune or that he was forced to call a new one" (262). But he does not escape the individual publisher's vantage point enough to question what that "tune," old or new, might be. To think through the death of the three-decker novel we again need a more relational, a dialectical point of view, not least because, as Gettmann admits,

> actually the 'nineties was not a bad time for publishers, as may be seen from the number of other new firms which came into existence and flourished at this time—Edward Arnold, Methuen and Company, John Lane, and Duckworth and Company. (263)

For the disappearance of the three-volume format, while sudden enough to be an "event," is by no means the cause of publishers not being able to "call the tune," but rather a symptom of what was a conjunctural crisis in the production of books, the result, as Gareth Stedman Jones says in another context, of "a temporary fusion of seemingly unconnected long-term and short-term phenomena."[3] The decline in the libraries' profitability, the appearance of new publishers, and the death of the three-decker are all determinate elements in that conjunctural crisis whose "short term," I would argue, extends from Frederick Macmillan's announcement in 1890 of a "net" pricing policy, through the Net Book Agreement of 1899 and the "*Times* Book War" of 1906-8, to the inclusion, in 1914, of fiction under the Net Book Agreement. Such empirical observations as that there was a new "buyers' market" in books, or that "the subscription-and rental-library trade . . . was being re-established on a more popular basis," or that "the whole price structure was revised downward,"[4] can take their meaning only in relation to an explanation of that wider crisis.

Griest's account, full as it is of detail, is weakened by her empiricist analysis, which simply allows, it seems, Time to solve all the publishers' difficulties she describes. She mentions the reactions of the interested parties to Mudie's decison, in June 1894, to accept no more three-volume novels, the London Booksellers' Society's endorsement of Mudie's action, the fears of the Society of Authors, and the responses of various publishers, concluding with the "complete and objective" analysis of a correspondent to the *Pall Mall Gazette* (176-88). But neither the *Gazette's* analyst at the time nor Griest attempts to analyze the demise of the three-decker in its relations to the whole structure of the production of novels in Victorian England. Yet the three-decker had been an integral part of that structure; for the previous half-century or more, the hegemonic structure in novel production had been the initial publication of expensive three-volume novels which were then discounted to the lending libraries, which circulated them to members at a shilling a volume, with cheap reprints in any form being delayed, usually for a year. This production of commodity-books had guaranteed safe profits on all levels, retail book-sellers profiting as well on the sale of the eventual reprints of successful novels. Any one of these structural elements admitted variations; a publisher might also adopt the alternative mode of part-issue, or discounts might vary, or reprinting might occasionally occur somewhat sooner, but the combination of a high list price, discounts to the libraries, multiple volumes, and the delay in reprinting, supported by an ideological consensus including the novel-reading public, this set of relations provided the dominant petty-commodity structure of novel production and was seen generally as how novels were best to be produced. Because none of the standard accounts sees this as a structure, the significance of the sudden extinction of the three-decker is obscured or sentimentalized, as it was for his contempories by Kipling's poem, which eulogizes the three volume novel as a sort of peaceful "Téméraire":

> . . . spite all modern notions, I found her first and
> best,
> The only certain packet for the Islands of the
> Blest.[5]

But what was occurring was not the arrival of "modern notions" but rather a radical transformation of the literary mode of production, the historical appearance of a new kind of structure, suited to, demanded, and provided by the larger structures of emergent monopoly capitalism.

The signs of confusion were everywhere in the publishing industry from the mid-80s. The era of "free trade in books," inaugurated in 1852 by the defeat of the London Booksellers' Committee's attempt to regulate retail prices, had been a period of intense retail price competition, as booksellers discounted new books directly to the public. Indeed, because of this, by 1890, when the London Booksellers' Society was founded, "the complete collapse of retail bookselling" seemed imminent.[6] At the same time, the circulating libraries' profits were diminishing because the number of novels published (and the space required to stock three-deckers) was increasing faster than the subscription lists, a pressure that was increased as the publishers more often hurried the date of reprinting at a low price.[7] Individual authors such as George Moore demanded that novels be issued at "a purchaseable price," so that they might appeal directly to the public, while authors organized into the Society of Authors in 1883, a move which was thought to be provocative, "trade union" behavior.[8] The Education Act of 1870 had obviously changed the conditions of publishing, as did the Berne Convention on international copyright in 1887 and the American "Chace Act" of 1891:

> The decline of the three-decker from the mid-eighties until its death in the mid-nineties is well known to have resulted from differences between British publishers, booksellers, circulating libraries and the Authors' Society. But it is not altogether fanciful to detect a contributory cause in American copyright law. After 1891 the British publisher was naturally reluctant to go to the expense of printing three volumes at home of a novel which had also to be manufactured as a single volume in America.[9]

From the point of view of the production of books those are but contributions or responses to the larger, conjunctural crisis; the prevailing arrangement, the relations of production and distribution, were clearly blocking realization of the potential for the production of commodity-texts. The crisis entailed changing the system while retaining control; the problem was who was to inherit control of the production of books, and the answer, of course, was the capitalist publishers.

This is not to say that the publishers conspired to establish a new hegemony. Just as Mudie's decision in 1894, and the concurrence of W. H. Smith, had been decisions on the level of "the firm"—Arthur Mudie had written to Bentley that the three-volume novel "serves no useful purpose whatever in our business"[10]—so the decision in 1890 to enforce "net" prices on books had initially been that of one firm, Macmillan (indeed of one man, Frederick Macmillan), and had been addressed specifically to "the evils of underselling and to the possibilities of curing them."[11] A good deal of the ideological strength of Macmillan's proposal in his 6 March 1890 letter to *The Bookseller* derived simply from his invoking "the rationality of the individual firm."[12] As he explained in his letter, Macmillan acted in response to "a number of private communications" from booksellers, and his course of action was to be entirely within the rights of an individual firm. He proposed "a general reduction of retail prices, and the diminution of trade allowances to such a point that the full published ["net"] price may reasonably be demanded and obtained from purchasers," with the further stipulation that Macmillan and Co. would allow trade terms (i.e. even the "diminished" trade allowance) only to "booksellers who would undertake not to break prices."[13] Thus, unlike the booksellers' scheme of forty years earlier to enforce existing high prices by collectively boycotting undersellers, Macmillan's plan satisfied the ideological norms of "free trade," by first enabling him to lower the artificially high price of his books, and by then allowing him to do business only with those booksellers whom he chose. Moreover, initially not all books were to be sold "net"; some were to be sold as "subject" books, subject, that is, to discounting by the bookseller, so that, here too, the charge of an unwarranted, total control was evaded. The crucial managerial decisions as to which books were to be sold "net," and which "subject," were of course, to rest with the publisher (this power was to allow the entrepreneurial experimentation of the next two decades, to which I shall return later). Macmillan's action in the 1890s was not collusive but exemplary, and when his carefully calculated risk in selecting Alfred Marshall's *Principles of Economics* as his first net book proved as successful as he had hoped, other publishers also were prepared to set net prices for books. In 1895 the Associated Booksellers of Great Britain and Ireland was founded (succeeding the London Booksellers) "to support . . . the principle of a net price for books."[14] The Publishers' Association was formed in the same year, and by 1899 the Net Book Agreement had been adopted by the two associations and by the Society of Authors and went into effect the next year.[15] The Net Book Agreement had established a new, consensual "terms of trade"; Frederick Macmillan proudly referred to it in 1924 as "the Magna Charta of the book trade."[16]

But if the Net Book Agreement was the book trade's Magna Charta, the "Book War" was its war of liberation, the struggle by which the new publishing structure established itself ideologically. That controversy from 1906 to 1908 over the practices of the *Times* Book Club both clarified the new terms which the agreement had instituted and showed that they could be defended publicly, that the new ideological consensus was one which not even the *Times* could subvert. The *Times* had been in financial difficulty in the early 1900s: for several years neither its sales, the amount of advertising, nor its profits had grown. Moberly Bell, its editor, believed that it had become impossible to make the *Times* pay, both because he believed that it was increasingly difficult to make even an ordinary newspaper pay and because the *Times* "was neither an ordinary newspaper nor produced in ordinary conditions."[17] In 1898, assisted by two American entrepreneurs, Bell had attempted to boost circulation by marketing a cheap reprint of the ninth edition of the *Encyclopaedia Britannica* in installments. When this scheme proved profitable, the same promoters founded the *Times* Book Club, a subscription system in which a "discount subscriber" to the *Times* might borrow any book, three volumes at a time, delivered and collected without charge anywhere in London. Also, and this was the real issue of the "Book War," the subscriber-member was entitled to purchase at a large discount any book previously borrowed.[18] Clearly, this promise to discount "unspoilt" copies a few weeks after publication side-stepped the Net Book Agreement; as a publishers' pamphlet argued, "a 'spoiled' copy is everywhere recognized as a copy which . . . cannot be sold as a new or fresh copy," and "an 'unspoilt' copy is, therefore, equivalent to a new copy."[19] Edward Bell, the president of the Publishers' Association, stated their case:

> It is obvious that such announcements were calculated to divert custom from the regular dealers in new books, and in the case of net books, amounted to an evasion, if not an actual infringement of the Net Book Agreement.[20]

The *Times,* of course, tried to define the terms of the struggle in its own interest:

> Fifty-four years ago the publishers attempted, by restrictions on trade, to maintain the high prices then charged for books, and to create for their own profit a firm and permanent monopoly, to be maintained at the expense of the public.
> Today the publishers . . . are trying to control not only the price of new books, but the price of second-hand books.[21]

But the prices were no longer "high," and the issue was no longer perceived as "monopoly"; the new terms of trade constituted by the Net Book Agreement seemed untouched by the *Times'* charges that while they did not formally constitute a trust they nevertheless allowed the publishers to be "so solidly organized that they act as against all outsiders with the unanimity and precision of a trust."[22] "Exclusive dealing" was the term helpfully suggested by the judge in the libel case which so undermined the position of the *Times* and its Book Club.[23] The Booksellers' Association and the Society of Authors[24] sided with the publishers, and when Lord Northcliffe secretly bought the *Times* in 1908 he quickly sued for peace. The settlement not only reasserted the Net Book Agreement "without any modification," but added a provision for a "close time" on Book Club copies, six months on net books and three months on subject books, during which they might not be sold as "second-hand." Thus ended, as Frederick Macmillan recalls, "in a manner most satisfactory to me and to publishers in general, one of the most remarkable quarrels in the annals of the Book Trade."[25] The satisfactory result was to establish the Net Book Agreement definitively as the "terms of trade," and thus to allow the victorious publishers fully to explore the possibilities in these newly structured relations of production and distribution of books.

But what had happened in the book trade was simply what had happened generally in the production and distribution of commodities at the turn of the century. The end of the last and the beginning of the new century, says a standard history of the subject, "saw a decisive change from competitive to associative organization in almost every trade in Britain," as a new form of monopolist organization established itself in retail trade associations like the Publishers' Association. This was "merely a continuation of the development of cartels and trusts in British industry,"[26] in the same way that the Net Book Agreement transformed the hegemony of the three-decker/lending library arrangement by concentrating control in the hands of publishers. The purpose of the agreement (indeed, the "kernel" of all trade associations' policy) was "to eliminate certain phases of competition by imposing on their members certain regulations of trading,"[27] that is, to eliminate "underselling" by enforcing net prices for books. But the practices of retail price maintenance have a more direct bearing on our understanding of publishing practice following the Net Book Agreement. Hermann Levy discusses the way that manufacturers, given "general agreement about price levels and certain trading conditions," are now constantly faced with the need to devise "new methods of securing [their] retailing customers," and a primary means is that extension of the principle of a *patent* which creates "branded goods," to be sold at advertised (or in the publishers' term, "net") prices.[28]

"Manufacturers," Levy writes, "have always been in search of means of creating for their goods some reputation-value, apart from cheapness or quality":

> The manufacturer who wishes to exploit the mass demand of modern retail markets . . . must broaden the sphere of patented goods into a field where the quasi-monopolist feature is not made up by legal rights but by the reputation and good will which his article gains. . . . Generally the manufacturer finds it necessary to approach the consumer directly, and so to create for himself a reliable mass market of the "unknown" customer. If this end is achieved the relationship between manufacturer and retailer may be reversed; it is the manufacturer who by controlling this article of reputation has gained the upper hand.[29]

In the case of publishing, the "legal rights" Levy refers to might be compared to the old arrangement with the lending libraries. But in the new "direct" arrangement, control has passed to the publishers; "the key to the situation," writes another commentator, "lies in the manufacturer's hands."[30] The practice of "branded goods" permits manufacturers not only to "discipline price cutters"[31] but, more importantly, directly "to capture the retailer's customers" by creating what these economic historians call "consumer insistence": "it is this 'consumer insistence' which is intended to create the quasi-monopoly value of the brand."[32] Thus, while publishing may be "a type of business distinct from others in many respects,"[33] in many other respects it is very similar, these practices of retail price maintenance generally explaining the early distinction between "net" and "subject" books, the dynamics of book production under the Net Book Agreement, and the reasons for finally including, in 1914, novels among net books. Since the economics of the "branded article" conform fundamentally with "the necessities of modern mass distribution in general,"[34] in book publishing the "branded article" may be seen as a translation of the function of "class" categories in the "new journalism," interpellating "consumer insistence" from a "class" of "un-

known customers." The translation, the ideological categories, and the practices specific to book production may be
seen only occasionally in the few historical studies, but quite
vividly in publishers' notices in the trade journals of the
1890s and early 1900s.

Alfred Marshall's *Principles of Economics* ("2 vols. 8vo. Vol
I. price 12 s. 6 d. net"), the first net book published by
Macmillan, was announced in the *Bookseller* for 7 August
1890, five months after Frederick Macmillan had made his
plan public.[35] During the approach to Christmas 1890, Macmillan offered several more net books of various kinds, with
different formats and prices: Lockyer's *Meteoric Hypothesis*
(demy octavo, 17 s. net) and Bowdler Buckton's *Monograph
of the British Cicadae* (2 vols., vol 1, 33/6 net) on 1 November,
and then on 15 November two expensive, large paper,
super royal 8vo. limited editions: Mrs. Oliphant's *Royal
Edinburgh* and a reprint of *The Vicar of Wakefield* with 150
illustrations.[36] On 15 December, Macmillan listed a similar,
seven-guinea limited edition and then, in the Christmas
number of the *Publishers' Circular*, they advertised a *Library
Reference Atlas of the World* (£2. 12 s. net), some reprinted
works by Lewis Carroll at 2/6, 4s., 4/6, and 7/6 (all net) and a
"pocket edition" of Tennyson's *Poetical Works,* morocco
binding, gilt edges, 7/6 net.[37] From August 1890 to January
1891, Macmillan had introduced about twenty net books, in
various formats at different prices.[38] By April 1891, Heinemann was also advertising net books, and in August 1891
Cassell's announced with some fanfare a "new library of
popular works at a 'net price,' to be known as 'Cassell's
International Novels.' "[39] This last venture seems to have
been premature, perhaps one of that firm's "miscalcula-
tions" at that period, for by Christmas 1892 all of the novels
in the series, originally priced at 7/6 net, were advertised at
six shillings each, with no mention of net prices.[40]

We can see very clearly from this the trial and error
through which the system of book distribution was reconstituted in the interest of those who controlled production, the
publishers. At the inaugural dinner of the London Booksellers' Society in 1890, David Stott, in the chair, had called
Macmillan's recent proposal "a step in the right direction,"

but his notion of what "net books" might mean was limited by his bookseller's perspective:

> There are some books a bookseller cannot sell, and no persuasion or blandishment can influence the customer to buy them. I refer to books on special subjects—technical or specially scientific books, for instance, such as we only purchase when they are ordered. . . .
>
> But on the other hand I protest against any publisher attempting to do the same thing with cheap books. . . .[41]

And in 1894, the *Bookseller*, responding in "Trade Gossip" to letters to the *Times* about net book prices, was again to specify "the application of the system to certain select classes of books, especially those published at a high price, or which appeal only to a limited class of readers."[42] Macmillan's choice of net books in those early months was clearly to some extent dictated by those considerations; but their very first choice for a net book had been intended from the start to test a more subtle possibility. "It was important that the book chosen should be a good one," Frederick Macmillan recalled,

> because if the first net book did not sell, its failure would certainly be attributed to its *netness* and not to its quality. It so happened that in the spring of 1890, we had in preparation a book on *The Principles of Economics*, by Professor Alfred Marshall, the well-known economist and then Professor of Political Economy at the University of Cambridge. There was little doubt that this book would at once take a leading place in the literature of Economics, and it suggested itself as a most appropriate subject for the experiment we wished to try.[43]

Here we have the beginning of an experiment in selling books as a new kind of "branded goods"; rather than appealing to a known, limited market for a commodity-book, with Mrs. Oliphant's *Royal Edinburgh*, say, or to the market for gilt edges and morocco bindings, Macmillan is here testing an assumed "quality," a "reputation-value," as a way of interpellating the "unknown" reader prepared to buy a commodity-text. Books advertised as "net" in these first years appear to be of these two types: either they are the sort of books which David Stott and other booksellers could not sell generally, on abstruse topics or in special formats or bindings, or they are books which by some sort of "reputation-value" may be hoped to interpellate an unspecified "class" of unknown readers. Thus "net" books might be either commodity-books or commodity-texts; "subject" books remained commodity-books, subject ultimately to a bookseller's persuasion and blandishment, as well as discount. But it was the possibility of extra profit which was opened up in the "net" category which publishers were to explore and exploit directly.

To assert, then, that "at first the net system was only applied to high priced books, especially books selling at more than 6 *s.*," is inaccurate, but more importantly it is an assertion which arises out of "free market" assumptions, based on the simple efficacy of "demand." The net system was at first applied only to high-priced books, Russi Jal Taraporevala writes, "presumably because the demand for these books was considered by publishers to be relatively inelastic":

> Hence the increase in price, due to "netting," was not expected to reduce total sales substantially. On the other hand cheaper books, for which the demand was presumably thought to have been more elastic, came within the net system only in its later years.[44]

The problematic of a presumed elasticity/inelasticity of "demand" only obscures the dynamics of the net book system; from the point of view of the production of books (rather than "demand"), the publishers may be seen to have eventually so expanded net books as sophisticated "branded goods" that "demand" became a controlled effect of production. The "reputation-value" at the core of "branded goods" lay in an author's name, as with the "well-known" Professor Marshall, interpellating unknown readers of

commodity-texts, creating a new audience, although ideologically it might be explained as "satisfying a demand."
Publishers were now in a position in the economic structure
to undertake in a controlled way the creation of the kinds of
mass audiences which the different careers of Charles Dickens and Charles Knight, seventy-five years earlier, had
shown to be accessible to a new literary mode of production,
by exploiting systematically the power of a commodity-text
to interpellate an infinity of unknown subjects. Neither an
author, a printer, nor a bookseller could afford

> to take the risk of promoting books . . . on the
> scale that was now necessary. Older publishing
> houses . . . rose to greater prominence, and new
> ones . . . soon achieved leading positions in the
> book trade.[45]

Hence "the mad quest for the golden seller" that Henry
Holt described in "The Commercialization of Literature" in
1905, "the mad payment to the man who has once produced
it, and the mad advertising of doubtful books in the hope of
creating the seller."[46]

Raymond Williams has approached this moment of "a
bouncing cheeky finally rampant commercialism" from a
wholly different direction, concluding nonetheless that
"what happened between the 1890s and 1914 is of great
critical importance for the novel." He suggests that 1895,
the year in which Thomas Hardy stopped writing novels,
might serve to mark "a new situation in the English novel."
We can see at that time a "visibly altering world," an "emerging deciding dividing world," which manifests itself in the
history of the novel in the separating out of " 'individual' or
'psychological' fiction on the one hand and 'social' or
'sociological' fiction on the other," and in the coming of
"literature," that "working, working over, working through,
by the last of the great men, the last hero, the novelist."[47]
The editors of the *New Left Review*, interviewing Williams
nine years after he wrote this account, were uneasy with it,
pointing out that he did not really explore the reasons for
the decisive "caesura in the form of the novel."[48] If Williams,
in 1970, had been unwilling to associate the "disturbance"

with some system, "call it sociology or materialism or tech-nologico-Benthamism"[49] (F. R. Leavis's pejorative formulas in those years), in 1979 he is much more precise about "the political emergence of a new working class, and the cultural segregation of a new bourgeois order, after the 1880s." He speaks not only of the "very deep and successful reorganization of bourgeois cultural and educational institutions," "integrated and confident," insulated within "increasingly standardized and masculine institutions," but he specifies the apparatuses of these ideologies: educational institutions, "a fully extended bourgeois press," and "the modernization of publishing."[50]

It is there, indeed, in those apparatuses, that a materialist explanation of what is signified by the "caesura in the form of the novel" must be based. The particular forms of "modernization" I have been analyzing are not merely new "marketing techniques" but rather a necessary extension of the transformation of the relations of production which constituted fully capitalist book publishing. The process initiated in 1890 by Frederick Macmillan, explored in his own list and expanded to those of other publishers, was precisely the "emerging deciding dividing" process of which Williams writes. It arrives (in passing, of course), as net books become increasingly the rule, in increasingly integrated, confident, standardized, and masculine structures of capitalist control, "masculine" not only because of the list of agents (Macmillan, John Murray, William Heinemann, or Edward Arnold) but also because of the patriarchal necessity of control, of centralized, purposeful planning (sometimes described as "risk-taking") in the production of commodity-texts. For the disruptions in the form of the novel were produced by these transformations of the relations of novel production; if "the parting of the ways" (Williams's chapter heading in *The English Novel*) may be described on an ideal level as the separating of psychological from sociological fiction, from the point of view of production the separation was determined in the last instance by those very forces which determined the separation of "net" from "subject" books. Even new novels, until 1914 usually sold subject to discount, could not entirely escape "netness," those forces determining the overall net/subject structure, for the whole production process, as well as each sector of it, was inevitably in an overdetermined relationship to the "visibly altering world," the "quite fundamental changes in the economic situation," such as scientific management and the revival of capital export, which were producing also the new unionism, the crisis in the London housing market and in the growth of the suburbs, and, in 1903, the Women's Social and Political Union.[51]

Edward Arnold was one of the first of the new names in publishing in the nineties; although the firm became noted for publishing the standard school books required after the Education Act, fiction was "not uncommon under this imprint" early in the century.[52] Forster came to Arnold with *A Room with a View* in 1908. His first two novels had been published by William Blackwood. Forster had sent a short manuscript entitled "Monteriano" to *Blackwood's Magazine* in 1905 and, as he wrote to his mother, Blackwood offered to publish it in volume form:

> the terms they offer are not at all good—I have written trying to do better, and meantime am trying to find out whether Blackwoods as *publishers* are a good firm, as though I dont mind much about money it's important to be in the hands of people who will advertise you well. Methuen and Heinemann are the firms I should have naturally tried first. The title has to be changed, which is very sad, but I see their point of view.[53]

Blackwood's point of view was that the name "Monteriano" would be detrimental to the sale of the book; a friend of Forster's suggested "Where Angels Fear to Tread" and Blackwood agreed that the change would improve the novel's "already slight chances of success."[54] Forster remained with Blackwood for *The Longest Journey* (1907) but switched to Arnold with *A Room With a View*; the reasons for the change are unknown.[55] In March 1909 Forster sent Arnold a synopsis and "a rough draft" of thirty chapters of *Howards End*.[56] Oliver Stallybrass, the editor of the Abinger

Edition of the novels, notes that the firm's readers and Arnold himself were bothered by Helen's sexual encounter with Leonard Bast, perhaps having that episode in mind when they suggested shortening the novel. A month later, when the novel was in proof, Forster indicated to Arnold some agreement about Helen:

> I was much struck by your original criticism, and tried to do what I could, but the episode had worked itself into the plot inextricably. I hope however that the public may find the book convincing on other counts.[57]

Edward Arnold published *Howards End* on 18 October 1910, 6 *s.*, crown 8vo., in 2,500 copies with further impressions of 1,000, 3,000 and 2,500 copies in November 1910, and 1,000 more in December; 9,959 copies were sold.[58] P. N. Furbank describes the novel's reception: "The book hit the note of the time. . . . For the first time the word 'great' was bandied about . . .," and he quotes the *Daily Mail* reviewer's emphasis on the novel's "coherence and connectedness," saying that "only connect" might be Forster's motto "not only for his book but for his method of work":

> the fitting of the perception of little things with the perception of universal things; consistency, totality, *connection*. Mr. Forster has written a *connected novel.*[59]

Clearly one "note of the time" which *Howards End* hit is indicated by the appreciation in the contemporary press for the injunction to "connect," a note which paradoxically seems timeless, given the attention paid by later critics to Forster's concern with "the relationships, and the possibility of reconciliation, between certain pairs of opposites." For just as *A Room with a View* is said to have "resonated" with "interlocking sets of contrasting pairs," so in general Forster is seen to define problems "dualistically," to explore "dichotomies," to find "some new and fruitful antithesis by which to set his convictions in play," and in *Howards End* to unfold an Arnoldian "series of polarities."[60] What is significant is the ideological attraction, for contemporary and later critics alike, of Forster's project. In 1910-11 it was perhaps welcomed as a "liberal" response to perceived "real" divisions in society between "the democratic surface and the private core, the People and the people who counted," or between "individualism (and imperialism) as represented by the Conservative Party and collectivism as typified by the burgeoning labour movement," or between men and women.[61] Since then, as "liberalism" has declined as a public political stance, Forster's ideological position has been taken more privately, as "moral realism," or "judicious imperturbability," a "whole style of patient, synoptic comment on social issues."[62] *Howards End* thus develops its epigraph thematically in its repeated reference to Matthew Arnold's advice to see life steadily and see it whole, and this moral effort is further associated with the place, Howards End, one of "these English farms" where, "if anywhere, one might see life steadily and see it whole, group in one vision its transitoriness and its eternal youth, connect—connect without bitterness until all men are brothers."[63] This vision of connectedness is presented metaphorically again and again in *Howards End*, as when the narrator demonstrates the "wisest course" for showing a foreigner England: to stand on the summit of the final section of the Purbeck Hills, "then system after system of our island would roll together under his feet," and as Forster directs "the trained eye" to these systems,

> the reason fails, like a wave on the Swanage beach; the imagination swells, spreads and deepens, until it becomes geographic and encircles England. (164–65)

Yet such a vision, such imagination, is not accessible to the lower-middle-class Leonard Bast—in a moment of despair Leonard realizes "to see life steadily and to see it whole was not for the likes of him" (52)—nor was it available to a calculating businessman, "who saw life more steadily, though with the steadiness of the half-closed eye" (320). Margaret Schlegel, on the other hand, believing that it is impossible to see "modern life" steadily, had chosen "to see it whole" (158). The novel's "patient synoptic comment" is here vague and ambiguous, the imaginative vision which is its theme being finally only "an impossible, yet heroic, effort to 'see life steadily and see it whole,'"[64] which echoes both wistfully and a little shrilly in the defensive naiveté of its final words:

> "The field's cut!" Helen cried excitedly—"The big meadow! We've seen to the very end, and it'll be such a crop of hay as never!" (340)

But if Helen's outburst embodies the thematic uncertainty in *Howards End,* ignored or accepted by contemporary and later critics alike, its language, as in the final utterance, also embodies a more profoundly historical contradiction, in the novel's interpellation of its reader-subject. We, too, have "seen to the very end," of *Howards End*; but, then, who are "we"? The novel asks this question, historically crucial, on several levels, some of them more self-reflexive than others. "Who's 'we'?" Henry Wilcox asks his son, "My boy, pray, who's 'we'?" (281) and Wilcox is himself later asked by Margaret, as he is attempting to ensure her personal loyalty, "Who is 'we'?" (301). But in 1910 that question was central for the novelist too; it had a determinate historical weight. For while *Howards End* was published by Arnold "subject to discount," Longman, Chatto, and others were already publishing new fiction "net," in various formats and prices.[65] Forster was inevitably implicated in that continuing project to establish the new structures of net-book publishing; in 1909 he had joined with other authors in an undertaking "not to publish an edition of any novel first published at the price of 6 s. in a cheap form at any time within two years from the date of its first publication."[66] And whether a novel was published "net" or "subject," the reading audience as a whole was being reconstituted by the relations of production we have discussed. A novelist might not necessarily be attempting to interpellate a mass audience, but as the relations of production moved ever more towards that possibility it became increasingly difficult for a novelist to imagine who or where another, more specific audience might be. In *Howards End* this difficulty, the determinate presence of the Net Book Agreement, registers itself in the awkward indeterminacy of the narrator's indefinite pronouns, "we" and "one."

The characters in *Howards End* most often use the indefinite "we" in a conventional way, "in general statements in which the speaker includes those whom he addresses, his contemporaries, his fellow countrymen, or the like" (*OED*), as in Mrs. Munt's "what *we* are doing in music" (33), or sometimes by asserting a specifically upper-middle-class "we," as when she wonders if the Wilcoxes are "our sort" (6). Similarly, within the created Schlegel world, "one knows what foreigners are" (12), "one" being "anyone of everybody, including (and in later language often specially meaning) the speaker himself" (*OED*); thus Mrs. Wilcox gently rebukes her son: "one doesn't ask plain questions" (19). But, outside the Schlegel/Wilcox world, the narrator's "we" or "one" is far less confident. It may include the speaker, fellow countrymen, and the like, but the "like" may shift uneasily to include unknown reader/subjects. The narrator's "we" is often clearly English, as when the London railway termini are described as "our" gates to the provinces (9), or when "two members of our race" play at "Capping Families" (18). But while "we" are also occasionally clearly upper-middle-class—"we" visit the country on weekends, and "we" look back with disquietude to the "elder race" which once lived there (266)—the interpellation of that class is often undercut, complicated by a not-quite-assured irony which in its uncertainty acknowledges values and subjects more inclusive and urgent than class-values and class-subjects. Leonard Bast's flat in Camelia Road contains a photograph of "a young lady named Jacky" which had been taken "at the time when young ladies named Jacky were often photographed with their mouths open." Jacky's photograph and smile are condescended to further, but then the tone is disrupted just as the narrator moves directly to enlist the reader:

> Take my word for it, that smile was simply stunning, and it is only you and I who will be fastidious, and complain that true joy begins in the eyes, and that the eyes of Jacky did not accord with her smile, but were anxious and hungry. (46)

Who, indeed, constitute the "you and I" here, revised from the "you or I" of the manuscript precisely to be inclusive?[67] The narrator is, at first, still ironical about the "stunning" smile, then, as "you and I" is introduced, "fastidious" (and still more ironically "captious" in the manuscript [43]), but then erases "our" ironic privilege by admitting it, as "we" contradictorily acknowledge the anxiety and hunger. At a moment like this the text's "we," the "everybody" which includes "anybody," tries jerkily to expand to include even nobodies like Jacky.

There are other such moments of narrative uncertainty, where "our" uneasiness about who "we" are is signaled by a contradictory indefiniteness or a limp gesture towards inclusiveness.[68] The description, or more accurately the narrator's appropriation, of Helen's experience of "panic and emptiness" in Beethoven's Fifth Symphony concludes with the comment, when "Beethoven chose to make all right in the end," that "that is why one can trust Beethoven when he says other things" (31-32). The shift to the present tense marks the intensity of the interpellation of "one," yet the confidence of that interpellation is immediately dissipated by the indefinite openness of "other things"; "one" (everybody) can trust Beethoven, the text seems to say, so long as that "one" is prepared to grant "one" (anyone) a blank check.[69] A similar contradictory pull disrupts the opening sentences of Chapter 6: "We are not concerned with the very poor. They are unthinkable and only to be approached by the statistician or the poet" (43). Here the "we" is simply the community of narrator and present reader, but "unthinkable" intrudes again a class position which then quickly is softened by being deferred, placed within the thematic dualism of reason and imagination. But the whole of the structure of Chapter 6 is fraught with the indefiniteness of the audience whom the narrator attempts to interpellate. The chapter addresses precisely the division between rich and poor, "gentlefolk" and "the abyss," and how Leonard Bast is placed between them—Leonard "stood at the extreme verge of gentility. He was not in the abyss but he could see it" (43)—but more importantly the chapter struggles formally with how this division is to be thought. In his flat in

Camelia Road Leonard begins to read Chapter 2 of the second volume of *The Stones of Venice,* the "famous" chapter (46) in which Ruskin crosses the lagoon to the islands of Torcello and Murano, and as Leonard listens to "the rich man speaking . . . from his gondola" (46)—"Was there anything to be learned from this fine sentence? Could he adapt it to the needs of daily life?" (47)—the narrator points out the irrelevance of Ruskin to Leonard's daily life. With all its command of "admonition and poetry" (46),

> the voice in the gondola rolled on, piping melo-
> diously of Effort and Self-Sacrifice, full of high
> purpose, full of beauty, full even of sympathy
> and the love of men, yet somehow eluding all that
> was actual and insistent in Leonard's Life. For it
> was the voice of one who had never been dirty or
> hungry, and had not guessed successfully what
> dirt and hunger are.(47)

What is at first striking in this passage is how the narrator constructs a "Ruskin" so as to imply by contrast, however indistinctly, the desired attitude to the poor; whoever the interpellated subject may be, it is first of all to be distinguished from the text's "Ruskin" ("well-fed Ruskin" in the manuscript [43]). The textual revisions show how the necessary "Ruskin" was constructed: the original voice of "a man who had never guessed what dirt and hunger feel like" (and earlier, "what such sensations may be") is rewritten so that not only are "feelings" and "sensations" replaced by what dirt and hunger "are," but "a man" is generalized to the almost indefinite "one," who may have "not" (instead of "never") guessed these realities. The text has thus moved away from an imagined Ruskin's personal experience to the question of an attitude, the attitude of a less definite "one," perhaps including the reader or the narrator, who had not yet but might still guess successfully what are the actualities of a life like Leonard's.

The chapter continues for a paragraph, alternating Leonard's reading of Ruskin's aesthetic aspirations with the narrator's commentary. Jacky then returns to the flat and after their supper of cheap, ersatz food the chapter concludes with Leonard going back to finish his chapter of *The Stones of Venice:*

> Ruskin had visited Torcello by this time, and was ordering his gondoliers to take him to Murano. It occurred to him, as he glided over the whispering lagoons, that the power of Nature could not be shortened by the folly, nor her beauty altogether saddened by the misery, of such as Leonard. (53)

Again, the text's discordances, as well as the effort of revision, trace the struggle to interpellate a broadly inclusive vantage point for an unknown subject. Ruskin, in his own sentence about "the power of Nature," had spoken of "the misery of man," his gondola having passed the principal cemetery of Venice.[70] Forster had changed "man" to "Leonard" in the three earlier versions of this paragraph, but each time he had also included a phrase, finally deleted, about Ruskin's meditation: ". . . and this comforted him"; ". . . and he was comforted"; "this comforted him" (manuscript, 49, 50). To have retained this final phrase would have heightened the anomaly of "Leonard" in Ruskin's sentence because it would have pointed the text back to Ruskin's supposed feelings. What the text now does, instead of focusing ironically on a cheaply comforted Ruskin, is to conclude its effort to construct a subject-position, different from Ruskin's, from which one might think the almost unthinkable predicament of "such as Leonard," a position which interpellates an unknown subject, with indistinct class predispositions: gentlefolk perhaps, or those obliged to pretend they are gentlefolk, or those who are neither, but merely "unknown."

This effort which the text of *Howards End* so often makes tentatively to open up the narrator's "we," or the indefinite "one," to an "anyone" of a determinedly inclusive "everybody," is much more historically specific than being merely "the fag-end of Victorian liberalism."[71] It is the effort which the new literary mode of production demands of "net" books, but also of "subject" books (like most novels in 1910), as the new literary market is itself "produced." For while

Forster assuredly did not set himself in 1909-10 to write a best-seller in *Howards End,* he nevertheless equally surely wrote within a determinate structure of book production, developed over the preceding twenty years, which enabled publishers to use the new means of production to produce commodity-texts. The "bestsellerism" and "bestsellerdom" to which John Sutherland refers are but ideological labels for the full development in capitalist book production of that internal drive towards "total commercial rationalization" and the "hectic change and turnover" in which capitalism realizes its "general formula."[72] Sutherland finds "good historical reasons" why the modern novel is "necessarily tied to the wheels of progressive technology, commercial management and the dictatorship of the consumer."[73] I have denied the "dictatorship" of the consumer, insisting instead on the control of the capitalist publisher, but otherwise I have detailed the material conditions of Sutherland's necessities and traced that historical process in a text, not even of a best-seller, but of *Howards End.* For the audience of the old, hegemonic literary mode of production had disappeared with the three-decker; readers were being reagglomerated as "consumers" of commodity-texts by the new, rampant, fully capitalist literary mode of production, with the publishers' sway stretching past the bookseller to "capture the retailer's customers." And because these powerful lines of control extended themselves through the production process the interpellated subject was also transformed. Whatever Forster's political or social "liberalism," whatever its placement within Edwardian ideology generally, the reader addressed by *Howards End,* that novel's peculiarly indistinct interpellated subject, was inevitably determined by these material relations of its production. In the ambiguity of its constructed reader-subject *Howards End* bears the impress of its historical mode of production, encodes within itself, in the ways we have seen, its own record of "how, by whom and for whom it was produced."[74]

Notes

PREFACE

1. Nicos Poulantzas, *Political Power and Social Classes*, trans. T. O'Hagen (London: Verso, 1975), 13–16.

2. Terry Eagleton, *Criticism and Ideology* (London: NLB, 1976), 77.

3. Louis Althusser, "Ideology and Ideological State Apparatuses," *Lenin and Philosophy*, trans. B. Brewster (London: NLB, 1971), 182.

4. Karl Marx, *Capital*, trans. B. Fowkes (Harmondsworth: Penguin, 1976), 1:138.

5. Eagleton, *Criticism and Ideology*, 48.

6. Pierre Macherey, *A Theory of Literary Production*, trans. G. Wall (London: Routledge and Kegan Paul, 1978), 19.

CHAPTER ONE

1. George H. Ford, *Dickens and His Readers: Aspects of Novel Criticism Since 1836* (New York: Norton, 1965; 1955), 6; Richard D. Altick, *The English Common Reader: A Social History of the Mass Reading Public, 1800–1900* (Chicago: University of Chicago Press, 1957), 383–86; John Butt and Kathleen Tillotson, *Dickens at Work* (London: Methuen, 1957), 63-75.

2. See Louis Althusser, *Reading Capital*, trans. Ben Brewster (London: NLB, 1970), 28; Frederic Jameson, *Marxism and Form* (Princeton: Princeton University Press, 1971), x–xi.

3. J. Don Vann, "The Early Success of *Pickwick*," *Publishing*

History 2 (1977):51; Robert L. Patten, *Charles Dickens and His Publishers* (Oxford: Clarendon Press, 1978), 45.

4. See Ford, *Readers*, 5–6; Vann, "Early Success," 53, 51.

5. Patten, *Publishers*, 46; Ford, *Readers*, 12.

6. Patten, *Publishers*, 46.

7. Steven Marcus, "Language into Structure: *Pickwick* Revisited," *Daedalus* 101 (1972):189, 202 n.4.

8. Charles Dickens, *The Posthumous Papers of the Pickwick Club*, ed. Robert L. Patten (Harmondsworth: Penguin, 1972), 79; *"Pickwick Papers"* will refer to this edition, and subsequent page references will be incorporated into my text.

9. Terry Eagleton, *Criticism and Ideology* (London: NLB, 1976), 48.

10. "In petty commodity production . . . the producer remains owner of the product of his labour; he gives it up only in order to acquire for himself the goods which will ensure his existence. The division of labour has already separated the producer from his product, but it does not yet oppress the former by means of the latter." Ernest Mandel, *Marxist Economic Theory*, trans. B. Pearce (New York: Monthly Review Press, 1968), 1:66.

11. Barry Hindess and Paul Q. Hirst, *Pre-Capitalist Modes of Production* (London: Routledge and Kegan Paul, 1975), 304–5.

12. Gareth Stedman Jones, "Class Struggle and the Industrial Revolution," *New Left Review* 90 (1975):49; my italics.

13. E. J. Hobsbawm, *Industry and Empire* (Harmondsworth: Penguin, 1969), 40–41.

14. Louis James, "Economic Literature: The Emergence of Popular Journalism," *VPNL* 14 (1971):13; Leonard B. Schlosser, "The Graphic Confluence of 1800," *A Miscellany for Bibliophiles*, ed. H. George Fletcher (New York: Grastorf and Lange, 1979), 67–95.

15. Jones, "Class Struggle," 50.

16. Terry Belanger, "From Bookseller to Publisher: Changes in the London Book Trade, 1750–1850," in *Book Selling and Book Buying*, ed. Richard G. Landon (Chicago: American Library Association, 1978), 15.

17. Royal A. Gettmann, *A Victorian Publisher: A Study of the Bentley Papers* (Cambridge: Cambridge University Press, 1960), 1; John A. Sutherland, *Victorian Novelists and Publishers* (London: Athlone Press, 1976), 11.

18. Graham Pollard, "The English Market for Printed Books," *Publishing History* 4 (1978):34, 37.

19. Belanger, "Bookseller to Publisher," 12.

20. Patten, *Publishers*, 11; I shall return to this contrast in Chapter 3.

21. Gettmann, *Victorian Publisher*, 5,6; Sutherland, *Victorian Novelists*, 22, 23.

22. Sutherland, *Victorian Novelists*, 78, 80, 81.

23. Karl Marx, *Capital* (Harmondsworth: Penguin, 1976) 1:558; *Grundrisse* (Harmondsworth: Penguin, 1973), 735.

24. H. G. Aldis, "Book Production and Distribution, 1625–1800," *The Cambridge History of English Literature* (Cambridge: Cambridge University Press, 1914), 11:318.

25. Marx, *Capital*, 1:1017.

26. Sutherland, *Victorian Novelists*, 96.

27. James J. Barnes, *Free Trade in Books: A Study of the London Book Trade Since 1800* (Oxford: Clarendon Press, 1964), 2, 3.

28. Sutherland, *Victorian Novelists*, 27.

29. Augustine Birrell, *Seven Lectures on the Law and History of Copyright in Books* (South Hackensack, N.J.: Rothman Reprints, 1971; 1899), 10.

30. Philip Wittenberg, *The Protection and Marketing of Literary Property* (New York: J. Messner, 1937), 20; Lyman Ray Patterson, *Copyright in Historical Perspective* (Nashville: Vanderbilt University Press, 1968), 10.

31. Birrell, *Seven Lectures*, 93; see also Wittenberg, *Protection*, 22–23; Patterson, *Copyright*, 12; and Ian Parsons, "Copyright and Society," in *Essays in the History of Publishing in Celebration of the 250th Anniversary of the House of Longman, 1724–1974*, ed. Asa Briggs (London: Longman, 1974), 39.

32. Wittenberg, *Protection*, 11, 7; Patterson, *Copyright*, 13, Wittenberg, *Protection*, 7; Patterson, *Copyright*, 13.

33. Patterson, *Copyright*, 11; Wittenberg, *Protection*, 3–4; Patterson, *Copyright*, 16; Elizabeth Eisenstein rejects as "a dubious proposition" Arnold Hauser's rather vague assertion that "the idea of intellectual property" follows from the general "disintegration of Christian culture" rather than from "the beginnings of capitalism." Her own analysis demonstrates how "scribal culture" (a precapitalist literary mode of production) "worked against the concept of intellectual property rights." *The Printing-Press as an Agent of Change* (Cambridge: Cambridge University Press, 1979), 1:229 n. 186.

34. C. B. Macpherson, *Democratic Theory: Essays in Retrieval* (Oxford: Clarendon Press, 1973), 130; see also C. B. Macpherson, *The Political Theory of Possessive Individualism* (Oxford: Oxford University Press, 1962), 215, 231. I owe this reference to Macpherson to Pamela McCallum.

35. See, for example, Patten, *Publishers*, 21–27.

36. Contrast Eagleton, *Criticism and Ideology*, 51; this discussion

attempts to fill a perceived gap in Eagleton's "Categories for a Materialist Criticism" (chap. 2).

37. Pierre Macherey, *A Theory of Literary Production*, trans. Geoffrey Wall (London: Routledge and Kegan Paul, 1978), 42.

38. Roland Barthes, *S/Z*, trans. Richard Miller (New York: Hill and Wang, 1974), 20.

39. Jacques Derrida, "Living On: Border Lines," *Deconstruction and Criticism*, ed. Harold Bloom (New York: Seabury Press, 1979), 84.

40. Macherey, *Theory*, 53, 70; the "forces of literary production determine and are overdetermined by the modes of literary distribution, exchange and consumption." Eagleton, *Criticism and Ideology*, 47.

41. See Louis Althusser, "Ideology and Ideological State Apparatuses," in *Lenin and Philosophy*, trans. B. Brewster (London: NLB, 1971), 160–65; asserting that *"all ideology has the function* (which defines it) of 'constituting' concrete individuals as subjects" (170), Althusser goes on to explain the *process of constituting*, or "interpellation":

> It is indeed a peculiarity of ideology that it imposes (without appearing to do so, since these are "obviousnesses") obviousnesses as obviousnesses, which we cannot *fail to recognize* and before which we have the inevitable and natural reaction of crying out (alond or in the "still, small voice of conscience"): "That's obvious! That's right! That's true!" (172)

In this book I shall examine ways in which the various novels "impose obviousnesses as obviousnesses," interpellating or constituting their readers as subjects.

42. Macherey, *Theory*, 49; "If we are to make sense of the concept of structure it must be with the recognition that structure is neither a property of the object nor a feature of its representation" (40).

43. Jones, "Class Struggle," 49.

44. Altick, *Common Reader*, 260; Sutherland, *Victorian Novelists*, 11; James M. Brown has attempted a Goldmannian analysis of the importance of the ethos of the marketplace in Dickens's work: "the single most important organizing concept in the later work, and the core of the novels' social vision, is the obsessively recurring metaphor of society as one huge market-place." *Dickens: Novelist in the Market-Place* (London: Macmillan, 1982), 23.

45. Altick, *Common Reader*, 274.

46. Scott Bennett, "Revolutions in Thought: Serial Publication and the Mass Market for Reading," *The Victorian Periodical Press:*

Samplings and Soundings, ed. Joanne Shattock and Michael Wolff (Leicester: Leicester University Press, 1982), 226.

47. Scott Bennett, "John Murray's Family Library and the Cheapening of Books in Early Nineteenth Century Britain," *Studies in Bibliography* 29 (1976):140.

48. Bennett, "John Murray," 140, 141, 161, 162.

49. Bennett, "Revolutions in Thought," 242, 228, 248–51, 246.

50. "The fact was that Dickens' main audience, overwhelmingly the most numerous one, was the middle class"; Richard D. Altick, "Varieties of Readers' Response: the Case of *Dombey and Son,*" *Yearbook of English Studies* 10 (1980):73; "the general ideological profile [is] *bourgeois* rather than *popular* (plebian, democratic)," Darko Suvin, "The Social Addressees of Victorian Fiction: A Preliminary Enquiry," *Literature and History* 8 (1982):26.

51. Patten, *Publishers,* 71; unfortunately the list of questions which Patten poses in his Introduction works against seeing publication as the sort of "process" I am trying to analyze.

52. Ford, *Readers,* 10; Kathleen Tillotson, *Novels of the Eighteen-Forties* (Oxford: Clarendon Press, 1954), 26; Patten lists five kinds of "early serial publications," *Publishers,* 46.

53. Butt and Tillotson, *Dickens at Work,* 66.

54. Patten, Introduction, *Pickwick Papers,* 11.

55. Ibid., 12.

56. Tillotson, *Novels,* 26; Sutherland, *Victorian Novelists,* 21; see also "The Letter from Chapman and Hall to Dickens, 12 February 1836, Proposing Terms for *Pickwick Papers,*" in *The Letters of Charles Dickens,* ed. Madeline House and Graham Storey (Oxford: Clarendon Press, 1965), 1:Appendix C, 648.

57. Patten, *Publishers,* 64, 46, 47.

58. Patten, Introduction, *Pickwick Papers,* 12–13.

59. Tillotson, *Novels,* 32.

60. Patten, Introduction, *Pickwick Papers,* 15, 16.

61. Patten, *Publishers,* 69.

62. *Pickwick Papers,* Preface to the Cheap Edition, 1847, 44.

63. Duane De Vries, *Dickens' Apprentice Years: The Making of a Novelist* (Hassocks, Sussex: Harvester Press, 1976), 143.

64. Marcus, "Language into Structure," 189.

65. *Pickwick Papers,* Appendix A, 903.

66. Tillotson, *Novels,* 33.

67. Butt and Tillotson, *Dickens at Work,* 71.

68. Edward Said, *Beginnings: Intention and Method* (New York: Basic Books, 1975), 226.

69. *Pickwick Papers,* Appendix A, 900.

70. Sutherland, *Victorian Novelists*, 22.
71. Dickens, *Letters*, 1:648.
72. *Pickwick Papers*, Appendix A, 899.
73. De Vries, *Dickens' Apprentice Years*, 144.
74. F. S. Schwarzbach, *Dickens and the City* (London: Athlone Press, 1979), 1.
75. David Harvey, "Class-Monopoly Rent, Finance Capital and the Urban Revolution," *Regional Studies* 8 (1974):254.
76. Schwarzbach, *Dickens and the City*, 44.
77. Eagleton, *Criticism and Ideology*, 110 n. 26.
78. Ford, *Readers*, 8, 10.
79. Steven Marcus, *Dickens: From Pickwick to Dombey* (New York: Basic Books, 1965), 31, 35, 28.
80. See Alexander Welsh, "Waverly, Pickwick, and Don Quixote," *Nineteenth Century Fiction* 22 (1967–68):19–20.
81. Steven V. Daniels, "Pickwick and Dickens: Stages of Development," *DSA* 4 (1974):77.
82. Patten, Introduction, *Pickwick Papers*, 24.
83. J. Hillis Miller, *Charles Dickens: The World of His Novels* (Cambridge, Mass.: Harvard University Press, 1959), 34.
84. Marcus, "Language into Structure," 185.
85. Edgar Johnson, *Charles Dickens: His Tragedy and Triumph* (New York: Simon and Schuster, 1952), 1:156.
86. Said, *Beginnings*, 227.

CHAPTER TWO

1. Carl Dawson, *Victorian Noon: English Literature in 1850* (Baltimore: Johns Hopkins University Press, 1979); W. L. Burn, *The Age of Equipoise* (New York: Norton, 1965).
2. Trygve R. Tholfson, *Working Class Radicalism in Mid-Victorian England* (London: Croom Helm, 1976), 11.
3. *The Letters and Private Papers of W. M. Thackeray*, ed. Gordon N. Ray (Cambridge, Mass.: Harvard University Press, 1945–46), 3:47; hereafter referred to as *LPP*.
4. James J. Barnes, *Free Trade in Books* (Oxford: Clarendon Press, 1964), 28.
5. E. J. Hobsbawm, *Industry and Empire* (Harmondsworth: Penguin, 1969), 118.
6. Richard Altick, "English Publishing and the Mass Audience in 1852," *Studies in Bibliography* 6 (1954):17; Barnes, *Free Trade*, 30–32.
7. Letter to the Editor of the *Times* (30 March 1852) from

Longman, Brown & Co., and John Murray, *Publishers and the Public: Reprinted from The Times of 1852* (London: The Times, 1906), 6; this collection of letters, editorials, and reprints from *Hansard* hereafter referred to as *PPR*.

8. Barnes, *Free Trade*, 18, 17.

9. This paragraph summarizes Barnes, *Free Trade*, chap. 2, "The Bookselling Question of 1852."

10. Marjorie Plant, *The English Book Trade*, 3d ed. (London: Allen and Unwin, 1974), 276.

11. Barnes, *Free Trade*, 115.

12. John Sutherland, "The Institutionalization of the British Book Trade to the 1890s," in *Development of the English Book Trade, 1700–1899*, ed. R. Myers and M. Harris (Oxford: Oxford Polytechnic Press, 1981), 97.

13. John Chapman, "The Commerce of Literature," *Westminster Review* 1, n.s. (1 April 1852):531.

14. Sutherland, *Victorian Novelists*, 72.

15. Ibid., 11.

16. Joseph Shaylor, *The Fascination of Books* (London: Simpkin and Marshall, 1912), 159–60.

17. Chapman, "The Commerce of Literature," 519.

18. A. W. Pollard, "Commercial Circulating Libraries and the Price of Books," *Library*, 4th ser., 9 (1929):415.

19. Richard Altick, *The English Common Reader* (Chicago: University of Chicago Press, 1957), 263.

20. Sutherland, *Victorian Novelists*, 17.

21. *PPR*, 8.

22. Sutherland, *Victorian Novelists*, 13.

23. Graham Pollard, "The English Market for Printed Books," *Publishing History* 4 (1978):42.

24. John Carter, *Victorian Fiction: An Exhibition of Original Editions at 7 Albermarle St., London* (London: Cambridge University Press, 1947), 5; *Simpkins: Being Some Account of the Origin and Progress of the House of Simpkin, Marshall, Hamilton, Kent & Co., Ltd.* (London: 1924), 1.

25. Sutherland, *Victorian Novelists*, 25.

26. Royal A. Gettmann, *A Victorian Publisher: A Study of the Bentley Papers* (Cambridge: Cambridge University Press, 1960), 241.

27. Sutherland, *Victorian Novelists*, 68.

28. Ibid., 113.

29. Gettmann, *Victorian Publisher*, 232, 233.

30. Carter, *Victorian Fiction*, ix n. 2, 5.

31. Pollard, "Commercial Circulating Libraries," 415.

32. Guinevere Griest, *Mudie's Circulating Library and the Victorian Novel* (Bloomington: Indiana University Press, 1970), 48.

33. Ibid., 47, 46.

34. Sutherland, *Victorian Novelists*, 112–13.

35. Gettmann, *Victorian Publisher*, 244.

36. Griest, *Mudie's*, 50, 125–29, 36–37.

37. *LPP*, III, 24.

38. Gordon N. Ray, *Thackeray: The Age of Wisdom, 1847–1863* (New York: McGraw-Hill, 1958), 1:171–72.

39. Quoted in "Memoir of George Smith," *DNB* (London: Oxford University Press, 1921–22), 1:xiv.

40. Barnes, *Free Trade*, 179.

41. Sutherland, *Victorian Novelists*, 105, 106, 108; my account follows Sutherland but emphasizes the embodiment of "enterprising caution" in the commodity-form.

42. Edgar F. Harden, "The Writing and Publication of *Esmond*," *Studies in the Novel* 13 (1981):81.

43. Sutherland, *Victorian Novelists*, 107, 104.

44. Griest, *Mudie's*, 49.

45. Sutherland, *Victorian Novelists*, 109, 110, 112.

46. Gordon N. Ray, *The Buried Life* (Oxford: Oxford University Press, 1952), 96.

47. J. A. Sutherland, *Thackeray at Work* (London: Athlone Press, 1974), 86.

48. Gordon N. Ray, *Thackeray: The Uses of Adversity* (New York: McGraw-Hill, 1955–58), 1:13.

49. W. M. Thackeray, *The History of Henry Esmond*, ed. T. C. and William Snow (Oxford: Clarendon Press, 1909), 372. Page references in the text are to this edition, which reproduces the text and pagination of Saintsbury's *Oxford Thackeray* while it includes the Snows' useful notes and appendices.

50. This concept was part of Thackeray's political vocabulary: in the 1840s he had dismissed the Whigs as "trimmers" (Ray, *Uses*, 1:192) and he uses the concept in *Henry Esmond* (436).

51. John Sutherland, "Thackeray's Notebook for *Henry Esmond*," *Costerus* 2, n.s. (1974):200.

52. Jane Millgate, "History Versus Fiction: Thackeray's Response to Macaulay," *Costerus* 2, n.s. (1974):51.

53. Sutherland, "Thackeray's Notebook," 198.

54. Sutherland, "Thackeray at Work," 68.

55. W.M. Thackeray, "Lecture the Third: Steele," in *The English Humourists of the Eighteenth Century*, vol. 13 of *The Oxford Thackeray*, ed. G. Saintsbury (Oxford: Clarendon Press, 1922), 542–43.

56. Ray, *Uses*, 2:106.
57. Gordon N. Ray, *"Vanity Fair:* One Version of the Novelist's Responsibility," *Essays By Divers Hands,* n.s., 25 (1950):99.
58. Ann Y. Wilkinson, "The Tomeavesian Way of Knowing the World: Technique and Meaning in *Vanity Fair,*" *ELH* 32 (1965):371.
59. Wilkinson, "Tomeavesian Way," 376, 373.
60. W. M. Thackeray, *Vanity Fair,* vol. 11 of *The Oxford Thackeray* (Oxford: Clarendon Press, 1922), 590.
61. Sylvia Manning, "Incest and the Structure of *Henry Esmond,*" *Nineteenth Century Fiction* 34 (1979):194–213.
62. See Terry Eagleton, *Criticism and Ideology* (London: NLB, 1976), 68ff.
63. See Howard O. Brogan, "Rachel Esmond and the Dilemma of the Victorian Ideal of Womanhood," *ELH* 13 (1946):223–24.

CHAPTER THREE

1. *The George Eliot Letters,* ed. Gordon S. Haight (New Haven: Yale University Press, 1954–78), 5:145–46, 124, 127, 137; hereafter cited in the text by volume as *GEL.*
2. Gordon S. Haight, *George Eliot* (Oxford: Clarendon Press, 1968), 433–44; J. A. Sutherland, *Victorian Novelists and Publishers* (London: Athlone Press, 1976), 188–205; J. A. Sutherland, "Lytton, John Blackwood and the Serialization of 'Middlemarch,'" *Biblioteck* 7 (1975):98–104.
3. Haight, *George Eliot,* 420–43; Jerome Beaty, *Middlemarch from Notebook to Novel* (Urbana: University of Illinois Press, 1960); Stanton Millett, "The Union of 'Miss Brooke' and 'Middlemarch': a Study of the Manuscript," *JEGP* 79 (1980):32–57.
4. Sutherland, "Lytton," 98; Sutherland, *Victorian Novelists,* 205.
5. Sutherland, *Victorian Novelists,* 190, 198–99; Haight, *George Eliot,* 433.
6. Sutherland quotes Joseph Langford, Blackwood's manager, as making such imputations. *Victorian Novelists,* 201.
7. Terry Eagleton, *Criticism and Ideology* (London: NLB, 1976), 113.
8. Maureen Mackintosh, "Reproduction and Patriarchy," *Capital and Class* 2 (1977):122.
9. See Sheila Rowbotham, *Hidden From History* (London: Pluto Press, 1973); Carol Bauer and Lawrence Ritt, eds., *Free and Ennobled: Source Readings in the Development of Victorian Feminism* (Oxford: Pergamon Press, 1979); Barbara Kanner, ed. *The Women of*

England: From Anglo-Saxon Times to the Present (Hamden, Conn.: Archon/Shoestring, 1979); Mary Evans and David Morgan, *Work on Women: A Guide to the Literature* (London: Tavistock, 1979).

10. Bessie Rayner Parkes, *Essays on Women's Work*, 2d ed. (London: Alexander Strahan, 1865), 55.

11. A fine recent analysis of "the intimate, albeit embattled connection between George Eliot's social and aesthetic concerns and the nineteenth century debate on the woman question" is in Suzanne Graver, *George Eliot and Community* (Berkeley: University of California Press, 1984), 167–83.

12. Roisin McDonough and Rachel Harrison, "Patriarchy and Relations of Production," in *Feminism and Materialism*, ed. Annette Kuhn and Ann Marie Wolpe (London: Routledge and Kegan Paul, 1978), 16; Dorothy Smith, "Women, Class and Family," in *Socialist Register 1983,* ed. Ralph Miliband and John Saville (London: Merlin Press, 1983), 5.

13. Juliet Mitchell, *Woman's Estate* (New York: Vintage Books, 1973), 100, 101.

14. Ibid., 101.

15. Kate Millett, *Sexual Politics* (New York: Doubleday, 1970), 139.

16. The most useful discussion of these elements of Marian Evans's situation is Phyllis Rose, *Parallel Lives* (New York: Knopf, 1983), 192–237, 300 n. 23.

17. Erna Reiss, *Rights and Duties of English Women* (Manchester: Sherratt and Hughes, 1934), 20; Eugene A. Hecker, *A Short History of Women's Rights* (New York: G. P. Putnam's Sons, 1911), 121; see also Barbara L. S. Bodichon, *A Brief Summary in Plain Language of the Most Important Laws of England Concerning Women, Together with a Few Observations Thereon,* 3d ed. (London: Trubner and Co., 1869), 1–5. Marian Evans playfully labeled her friend, Sarah Hennell, "femme sole" in 1869, *GEL,* 5:67.

18. William Blackstone, *Commentaries on the Laws of England,* 4th ed. (London: John Murray, 1876), 1:421; Reiss, *Rights and Duties,* 59–92.

19. Reiss, *Rights and Duties,* 29–30.

20. Michal Peled Ginsburg, "Pseudonym, Epigraphs, and the Narrative Voice: *Middlemarch* and the problem of Authorship," *ELH* 47 (1980):543–44.

21. Richard Altick, "The Sociology of Authorship," *BNYPL* 66 (1962):392.

22. Gaye Tuchman and Nina Fortin, "Edging Women Out: Some Suggestions about the Structure of Opportunities and the Victorian Novel," *Signs* 6 (1980):309.

23. Smith, "Women, Class and Family," 14.

24. J. S. Mill, "The Subjection of Women," in *Collected Works of John Stuart Mill: Essays on Equality, Law, and Education*, ed. J. M. Robson (Toronto: University of Toronto Press, 1984), 21:340, 280, 317.

25. Magali Sarfatti Larson, *The Rise of Professionalism* (Berkeley: University of California Press, 1977), 6; "the term 'profession' is intrinsically bound up with a particular period of history and with only a limited number of nations in that period of history." Eliot Freidson, "The Theory of Professions: State of the Art," in *The Sociology of the Professions*, ed. Robert Dingwall and Philip Lewis (London: Macmillan, 1983), 26.

26. Larson, *Rise of Professionalism*, 81.

27. Ibid., 63 6n.

28. H. J. Perkin, *The Origins of Modern English Society, 1780–1880* (London: Routledge and Kegan Paul, 1969), 428.

29. Lee Davidoff, *The Best Circles* (London: Croom Helm, 1973), 24.

30. A. S. Collins, *The Profession of Letters: A Study of the Relation of Author to Patron, Publisher and Public, 1780–1832* (London: Routledge and Kegan Paul, 1928), 7.

31. Eliot Freidson, "The Futures of Professionalisation," in *Health and the Division of Labour*, ed. Margaret Stacey et al. (London: Croom Helm, 1977), 16–17; Freidson, "Theory," 27.

32. Freidson, "Theory," 20, 31.

33. Freidson, "Futures," 20, 22.

34. Ibid., 23; Larson, *Rise of Professionalism*, 74, 51.

35. Freidson, "Futures," 32; Larson, *Rise of Professionalism*, 61, 62, 63, 14.

36. Freidson, "Theory," 34.

37. Elaine Showalter, *A Literature of Their Own* (Princeton: Princeton University Press, 1977), 13, 19.

38. In a review of three novels for the *Westminster Review* in 1856; *Essays of George Eliot*, ed. Thomas Pinney (London: Routledge and Kegan Paul, 1963), 334.

39. Showalter, *A Literature*, 48.

40. Ibid., 39; Tuchman and Fortin, "Edging Women Out," 320; "major women novelists of the nineteenth century stood on the margins of power sensing in themselves unused capacities for participation." Smith, "Women, Class and Family," 23.

41. Elaine Showalter, "Dinah Mulock Craik and the Tactics of Sentiment: A Case Study in Victorian Female Authorship," *Feminist Studies* 2 (1975):6.

42. Showalter, "Craik," 6; Sutherland also states that "the ques-

tion of the 'dignity' of *Middlemarch* weighed heavily with George Eliot and Lewes." *Victorian Novelists,* 199.

43. Showalter, *A Literature,* 53, 21.

44. George Levine, "Repression and Vocation in George Eliot: A Review Essay," *Women and Literature* 7 (1979):3; Karl Marx, *The Eighteenth Brumaire of Louis Bonaparte* (New York: International Publishers, 1963), 15.

45. *GEL,* 2:431.

46. R. F. Anderson, "Negotiating for *The Mill on the Floss,*" *Publishing History* 2 (1977):27; Haight, *George Eliot,* 369; Susan M. Greenstein writes of George Eliot's "increasingly commercial way of looking at her efforts." "The Question of Vocation: from *Romola* to *Middlemarch,*" *NCF* 35 (1981):495.

47. R. F. Anderson, " 'Things Wisely Ordered': John Blackwood, George Eliot, and the Publication of *Romola,*" *Publishing History* 11 (1982):11.

48. Anderson, "Negotiating," 27, 30–31.

49. Ibid., 30, 33, 34.

50. Ibid., 30.

51. Ibid., 35–36.

52. Greenstein, "The Question of Vocation," 495.

53. Anderson, "Things Wisely Ordered," 14, 18, 23.

54. *GEL,* 3:339.

55. Greenstein, "The Question of Vocation," 493.

56. *GEL,* 4:38.

57. *GEL,* 4:33.

58. Anderson, "Things Wisely Ordered," 23, 24.

59. *GEL,* 8:304.

60. *GEL,* 8:289; 4:49.

61. Sutherland, *Victorian Novelists,* 205.

62. *GEL,* 5:179–80.

63. Sutherland, *Victorian Novelists,* 199.

64. Alan Mintz, *George Eliot and the Novel of Vocation* (Cambridge, Mass.: Harvard University Press, 1978), 17.

65. F. R. Leavis, *The Great Tradition* (London: Chatto and Windus, 1948), 72, 74.

66. George Eliot, *Middlemarch,* 3 vols. (Edinburgh: William Blackwood and Sons, 1871–72), 4:369–70; all page references in the text are to this edition.

67. Millett, "Union," 32, 33; Beaty, *Notebook,* 35.

68. Millett, "Union," 33.

69. Beaty, *Notebook,* 9–11; J. C. Pratt is far less tentative in his comments on the similarities in the general preoccupations in the two stories, "cause and effect, the succession of events": "We can

hardly doubt that it was recognition of these correspondences that underlay George Eliot's decision to fuse the two stories." John C. Pratt and Victor A. Neufeldt, eds., *George Eliot's Middlemarch Notebooks* (Berkeley: University of California Press, 1979), 1.

70. Beaty, *Notebook*, 7, 9, 14.

71. Pratt and Neufeldt, *Notebooks*, xlii.

72. W. J. Harvey, "The Intellectual Background of the Novel: Casaubon and Lydgate," in *Middlemarch: Critical Approaches to the Novel*, ed. Barbara Hardy (London: Athlone Press, 1967), 28 n.3.

73. Beaty, *Notebook*, 29; Millett, "Union," 42.

74. Beaty, *Notebook*, 29, 23; Millett, "Union," 47–48, 32.

75. See Mintz, *George Eliot and Vocation*, 17–18.

76. Anna Theresa Kitchel, *Quarry For Middlemarch* (Berkeley: University of California Press, 1950), 7–10; Pratt and Neufeldt, *Notebooks*, xxxvi.

77. As well as in the introductions and notes to Kitchel, *Quarry*, and Pratt and Neufeldt, *Notebooks*, the use of these materials in *Middlemarch* has been discussed in Asa Briggs, " 'Middlemarch' and the Doctors," *Cambridge Journal* 1 (1948):749–62; C. L. Cline, "Qualifications of the Medical Practitioners of *Middlemarch*," in *Nineteenth Century Perspectives*, ed. Clyde de L. Ryals (Durham, N.C.: Duke University Press, 1974), 271–81.

78. Kitchel, *Quarry*, 22–23.

79. Ibid., 24, 26, 27, 28, 29 n. 60.

80. Pratt and Neufeldt, *Notebooks*, 24–26.

81. Ginsberg, "Pseudonym, Epigraphs and Narrative Voice," 550, 552; Derek Oldfield's discussion of free indirect discourse as an "equivalent" or "correlative" for George Eliot's "aim of combining emotional involvement and ironic criticism" ignores the ideological limitations of her ironic criticism. Derek Oldfield, "The Language of the Novel: the Character of Dorothea," in *Critical Approaches*, ed. Hardy, 82–84.

82. Friedson, "Futures," 32.

83. "It is evident . . . that to deny all British medical degrees to women,—not only to refuse them instruction, but to refuse to examine them if they have acquired knowledge elsewhere,—*is* most arbitrarily to prohibit all women, whatever their qualification, from practising medicine in the United Kingdon, except under legal pains and penalties." Sophia Jex-Blake, "Medicine as a Profession for Women," in *Woman's Work and Woman's Culture*, ed. Josephine Butler (London: Macmillan, 1869), 109.

84. Barbara Hardy, *Particularities: Readings in George Eliot*, (London: Peter Owen, 1982), 138, 140.

85. *GEL*, 2:227.

86. See Jerome Beaty, "The Text of the Novel: A Study of the Proof," in *Critical Approaches,* ed. Hardy, 59–60; William Myers, *The Teaching of George Eliot* (Leicester: Leicester University Press, 1984), 117.

CHAPTER FOUR

1. Matthew Arnold, "Copyright," *Complete Prose Works,* ed. R. H. Super, vol. 9, *English Language and Irish Politics* (Ann Arbor, Mich.: University of Michigan Press, 1960–77), 114; page references in the text are to this edition.

2. Matthew Arnold, "Up to Easter," *Prose Works,* ed. Super, 11:202.

3. W. A. Copinger, *The Law of Copyright in Literature and Art,* 3d ed. (London: Stevens and Haynes, 1893), 78–84.

4. Copinger, *Copyright,* 551–52.

5. See Sidney J. Low, "Newspaper Copyright," *National Review* 113 (1892):648–66, and the letters in response, *National Review* 114 (1892):855–64.

6. Scott Bennett, "Prolegomena to Serials Bibliography: A Report to the Society," *VPR* 12 (1979):3.

7. Joel H. Wiener, "Circulation and the Stamp Tax," *Victorian Periodicals: A Guide to Research,* ed. J. Don Vann and R. Van Arsdale (New York: MLA, 1978), 149.

8. Stanley Morison, *The English Newspaper* (Cambridge: Cambridge University Press, 1932), 270.

9. Alan Lee, "The Structure, Ownership and Control of the Press, 1855–1914," in *Newspaper History from the Seventeenth Century to the Present Day,* ed. George Boyce, James Curran, and Pauline Wingate (London: Constable, 1978), 118.

10. H. R. Fox Bourne, *English Newspapers* (London: Chatto and Windus, 1887), 2:252–3.

11. Alan J. Lee, *The Origins of the Popular Press in England, 1855–1914,* (London: Croom Helm, 1976), 54–63; the most succinct account is Ellic Howe, *Newspaper Printing in the Nineteenth Century* (London: privately printed, 1943).

12. A. E. Musson, "Newspaper Printing in the Industrial Revolution," *Economic History Review* 10–11 (1957–59):424–26; see also Ellic Howe, *The London Compositor* (London: The Bibliographical Society, 1947), chap. 17, "Disputes on London Newspapers, 1845–1852," and chap. 18, "News Compositors' Methods of Working, 1868–1894."

13. Fox Bourne, *English Newspapers,* 2:253.

14. Howe, *Newspaper Printing*, 43.

15. Allen Hutt, *The Changing Newspaper* (London: Gordon Fraser, 1973), 48.

16. Morison, *English Newspaper*, 267–75.

17. Fox Bourne, *English Newspapers*, 2:275ff.

18. Michael L. Turner, "The Syndication of Fiction in Provincial Newspapers, 1870–1939," (B. Litt. diss., Oxford University, 1968), 8, 13ff; Fox Bourne, *English Newspapers*, 2:257.

19. Lee, *Origins*, 104–17.

20. Arnold, "Copyright," 116.

21. Kathleen Tillotson, *Novels of the Eighteen-Forties* (Oxford: Clarendon Press, 1954), 30.

22. Graham Pollard, "Serial Fiction," in *New Paths in Book Collecting*, ed. John Carter (London: Constable, 1934), 262, 263.

23. John Sutherland, *Victorian Novelists and Publishers* (London: Athlone Press, 1976), 37.

24. *The Newspaper Press Directory and Advertiser's Guide*, 5th ed., ed. Charles Mitchell (London: C. Mitchell, 1856).

25. Thomas Hardy, General Preface to the Novels and Poems, Wessex Edition—1912, *Thomas Hardy's Personal Writings*, ed. Harold C. Orel (London: Macmillan, 1967), 44.

26. I mean to distinguish "class" from class, "class" to indicate the particular, constituted audience of a journal (a journalism historian's term), and class to signify a relative position in a social formation (a term in marxist social analysis).

27. Charlotte C. Watkins, "Edward William Cox and the Rise of 'Class Journalism,'" *VPR* 15 (1982):92; "Class Papers and Periodicals" were indexed in *Mitchell's Directory* from 1879 (Susan Gliserman, "Mitchell's Newspaper Press Directory, 1846–1907," *VPN* 4 [1969]:19).

28. Charles Morgan, *The House of Macmillan* (London: Macmillan, 1943), 61.

29. Fox Bourne, *English Newspapers*, 2:294ff.

30. Walter Besant, *The Pen and the Book* (London: T. Burleigh, 1899), 228.

31. Arlene M. Jackson, *Illustration and the Novels of Thomas Hardy* (Totowa, N.J.: Rowman and Littlefield, 1981), 21.

32. Lee, *Origins*, 121.

33. Morison, *English Newspaper*, 307.

34. Tony Bennett, "Text, Readers, Reading Formations," *Literature and History* 9 (Autumn 1983):216, 225.

35. Oscar Maurer, "My Squeamish Public: Some Problems of Victorian Magazine Publishers and Editors," *SB* 12 (1959):24.

36. Lee, *Origins*, 129.

37. Gordon N. Ray, *The Illustrator and the Book in England from 1790 to 1914* (New York: Pierpont Morgan Library, 1976), 97.

38. Mason Jackson, *The Pictorial Press: Its Origin and Progress* (London: Hurst and Blackett, 1885), 317; "No other method of engraving lends itself so easily to the rapid productions of the printing-press" (360).

39. Mason Jackson, *Pictorial Press*, 315, 317, 320–21.

40. Percy Muir, *Victorian Illustrated Books* (London: Batsford, 1971), 8.

41. Clement T. Shorter, "Illustrated Journalism: Its Past and Its Future," *Contemporary Review* 75 (1899):489.

42. Watkins, "Class Journalism," 92.

43. Anthony Smith, "The Long Road to Objectivity and Back Again: The Kinds of Truth we get in Journalism," in Boyce, Curran, and Wingate, *Newspaper History*, 168.

44. George Boyce, "The Fourth Estate: The Reappraisal of a Concept," in Boyce, Curran, and Wingate, *Newspaper History*, 27.

45. Morgan, *Macmillan*, 59.

46. T. P. O'Connor, "The New Journalism," *The New Review* 1 (October 1889):434, 425.

47. [T. Wemyss Reid], "Modern Newspaper Enterprise," *Fraser's*, n.s. 13 (June 1876):708.

48. O'Connor, "New Journalism," 423, 429.

49. Lee, *Origins*, 189, 121.

50. All further page references in the text, including those to *Tess of the D'Urbervilles*, will be to the *Graphic*, vol. 44, 1891.

51. Tony Bennett, "Reading Formations," 224.

52. Thomas Hardy, "Candour in English Fiction," *New Review* (1890), collected in *Hardy's Personal Writings*, ed. Orel, 130.

53. Janet Freeman, "Ways of Looking at *Tess*," *Studies in Philology* 79 (1982):317.

54. J. Hillis Miller, *Thomas Hardy: Distance and Desire* (Cambridge, Mass.: Harvard University Press, 1970), 51.

55. Terry Eagleton, "Thomas Hardy: Nature as Language," *Critical Quarterly* 13 (1971):160.

56. These terms are quoted from the ideologically "pictorial" analysis in Arlene M. Jackson, *Illustration*, 4, 107.

57. Ibid., 106.

58. Ibid., 106, 113.

59. Hardy, "Candour," 128.

60. Cf. Thomas Hardy, *Tess of the D'Urbervilles*, ed. J. Grindle and S. Gatrell (Oxford: Clarendon Press, 1983), 263, hereafter referred to as *Tess* (1983).

61. J. T. Laird, *The Shaping of Tess of the D'Urbervilles* (Oxford: Clarendon Press, 1975), 15, 190, quoting John Paterson, *The Making of the Return of the Native* (Berkeley: University of California Press, 1960), 168.

62. S. Gatrell, Editorial Introduction, *Tess* (1983), 75–76.

63. *Tess* (1983), 263.

64. Simon Gatrell, "Hardy, House-Style and the Aesthetics of Punctuation," *The Novels of Thomas Hardy*, ed. Anne Smith (London: Vision Press, 1979), 177.

65. Gatrell, "House-Style," 180.

66. Gatrell, Editorial Introduction, *Tess* (1983), 90.

67. *Tess* (1983), 263; see also Appendix 6, "Punctuation and Styling Variants," 594.

68. Tony Bennett, "Reading Formations," 255. Mary Jacobus, in "Tess's Purity," has analyzed in detail "the form of Hardy's compromise . . . implicit in the novel's subtitle, 'A pure Woman.' " *Essays in Criticism* 26 (1976):319.

69. An extension or corollary to the analysis I am attempting (not relevant, that is, to the status of the *Graphic*'s *Tess* as a commodity-text) would be to analyze the commodity-text which each of the excerpted episodes became, determined not only by the different "class" of the *Fortnightly* or *National Observer* but by the difference in genre, to rethink within a historical materialist problematic the questions raised in Suzanne Hunter Brown's " 'Tess' and *Tess*: an Experiment in Genre," *Modern Fiction Studies* 28 (1982):25–44.

70. Florence Emily Hardy, *The Early Life of Thomas Hardy* (London: Macmillan, 1928), 291.

71. Michael Millgate, *Thomas Hardy: A Biography* (Oxford: Clarendon Press, 1982), 305; Michael Millgate, *Thomas Hardy: His Career as a Novelist* (New York: Random House, 1971), 292.

72. Florence Hardy, *Early Life*, 291.

CHAPTER FIVE

1. Guinevere L. Griest, *Mudie's Circulating Library and the Victorian Novel* (Bloomington: Indiana University Press, 1970), 209–11.

2. Royal A. Gettmann, *A Victorian Publisher: A Study of the Bentley Papers* (Cambridge: Cambridge University Press, 1960), 257.

3. Gareth Stedman Jones, *Outcast London* (Harmondsworth: Penguin, 1976), 152.

4. Richard Altick, *The English Common Reader* (Chicago: University of Chicago Press, 1957), 313.

5. Quoted in Griest, *Mudie's*, 7, and Gettman, *Victorian Publisher*, 245.

6. W. G. Corp, *Fifty Years: A Brief Account of the Associated Book-sellers of Great Britain and Ireland, 1895–1945* (Oxford: Basil Blackwell, 1945), 3; see also David Stott, "The Decay of Bookselling," *Nineteenth Century* 36 (1894):932–38.

7. Arthur Waugh, *A Hundred Years of Publishing* (London: Chapman and Hall, 1930), 192; Griest, *Mudie's*, 169–70.

8. Gettmann, *Victorian Publisher*, 256; Griest, *Mudie's*, 189; John Goode has analyzed the place of the Society of Authors in the "more mystified ideology of literary production" in "The Decadent Writer as Producer," in *Decadence and the 1890s*, ed. Ian Fletcher (London: Edward Arnold, 1979), 117–21.

9. Simon Nowell-Smith, *International Copyright Law and the Publisher in the Reign of Queen Victoria* (Oxford: Clarendon Press, 1968), 82.

10. Quoted in Griest, *Mudie's*, 173.

11. Frederick Macmillan, *The Net Book Agreement 1899 and the Book War 1906–1908* (Glasgow: Robert Maclehose, 1924), 4.

12. For the place of this ideology in late Victorian economic thinking, see E. J. Hobsbawm, *Industry and Empire* (Harmondsworth: Penguin, 1968), 187f.

13. Macmillan, *The Net Book Agreement*, 6, 16.

14. W. G. Corp, *Fifty Years*, 5; the London Booksellers' Society had already, in 1894, submitted to selected publishers a memorial supporting net prices. Russi Jal Taraporevala, *Competition and Control in the Book Trade, 1850–1939* (Bombay: D.B.T. Taraporevala and Sons, 1969), 36.

15. R. J. L. Kingsford, *The Publishers' Association, 1896–1946* (Cambridge: Cambridge University Press, 1970), 5–17.

16. Macmillan, *The Net Book Agreement*, 30.

17. [Anon.], *The History of the Times*, vol 3, *The Twentieth Century Test, 1884–1912*, (London: The Times, 1947), 441.

18. *The History of the Times*, 443–48.

19. [Anon.], *"The Times" and the Publishers* (London: privately printed for the Publishers' Association, 1906), 11–12, 7.

20. Edward Bell, *"The Times Book Club and the Publishers' Association, an Account of the 'Book War' of 1906–1908,"* in Macmillan, *The Net Book Agreement*, 31.

21. [Anon.], *Publishers and the Public: Reprinted From the Times of 1852* (London: The Times, 1906), Note, 1.

22. [Anon.], *The History of the Book War: Fair Book Prices Versus Publishers' Trust Prices* (London: The Times, 1907), 36.

23. *John and A. H. Hallam Murray v. Walter and Others* (London: printed for private circulation, John Murray, 1908), 84.

24. The *Times* attacked novelists as "the curled darlings of the

fiction market [who] came forth from the lotos-land through the looking-glass where they dwell withdrawn from the vulgar battle of commerce, or emerged from the vapourous private Utopias wherein they excogitate phosphorescent millenniums." *The History of the Book War*, 32.

25. Macmillan, *The Net Book Agreement*, 75, 77.

26. Hermann Levy, *Retail Trade Associations: A New Form of Monopolist Organization in Britain* (London: Kegan Paul, Trench, Trubner and Co., 1942), 20, 7.

27. Ibid., 5.

28. Ibid., 63–64.

29. Ibid., 65–66.

30. B. S. Yamey, "The Origins of Retail Price Maintenance: A Study of Three Branches of the Retail Trade," *EJ* 62 (1952):528.

31. Yamey, "Origins," 527–28.

32. Levy, *Retail Trade Associations*, 67, 70.

33. Ibid., 15.

34. Ibid., 71.

35. *The Bookseller*, 383 (7 August 1890):869 (hereafter referred to as *B*, with number, date, and page).

36. *The Publishers' Circular* (1 November 1890):1450; (15 November 1890):1525 (hereafter referred to as *PC*).

37. *PC* (15 December 1890):1622; (Christmas Number, 1890):106, 108.

38. Ian Norrie says sixteen in 1890. F. A. Mumby and Ian Norrie, *Publishing and Bookselling*, 5th ed. rev. (London: Cape, 1974), 244.

39. *B*, 404 (Apr. 1891); *PC* (1 Aug. 1891), 917; Frederick Macmillan lists the publishers in 1891 who were publishing net books, in *The Net Book Agreement*, 18.

40. Simon Nowell-Smith, *The House of Cassell, 1848–1958* (London: Cassell, 1958), 188; *PC* (Christmas Number, 1892):98.

41. *B*, 395 (10 October 1890):1020.

42. *B*, 444 (6 November 1894):1021.

43. Macmillan, *The Net Book Agreement*, 14.

44. Taraporevala, *Competition and Control*, 54.

45. B. W. E. Alford, "Business Enterprise and the Growth of the Commercial Letterpress Printing Industry, 1850–1914," *Business History* 7 (1965):4.

46. Henry Holt, "The Commercialization of Literature," *Atlantic Monthly* 96 (1905):599; the Americans had been listing "best sellers" since 1895. Alice Payne Hackett, *70 Years of Best Sellers: 1895–1965* (New York: R. R. Bowker, 1967), 2.

47. Raymond Williams, *The English Novel from Dickens to Law-*

rence (London: Chatto and Windus, 1970), 129, 119, 121, 119–20, 137.

48. *Politics and Letters: Interviews with New Left Review* (London: New Left Books, 1979), 261–62.

49. Williams, *The English Novel*, 130.

50. *Politics and Letters*, 262, 263.

51. Maurice Dobb, *Studies in the Development of Capitalism*, 2d ed. (London: Routledge and Kegan Paul, 1963), 313; Asa Briggs, "The Political Scene," in *Edwardian England, 1901–1914*, ed. S. Nowell-Smith (London: Oxford University Press, 1964), 82; Hobsbawm, *Industry and Empire*, 191.

52. Mumby and Norrie, *Publishing and Bookselling*, 279, 347.

53. Oliver Stallybrass, Editor's Introduction, *Where Angels Fear To Tread*, Abinger ed. (London: Arnold, 1975), xi; *Selected Letters of E. M. Forster*, ed. Mary Lago and P. N. Furbank (London: Collins, 1983), 1:67.

54. Stallybrass, Editor's Introduction, *Angels*, xii; Lago and Furbank, *Letters*, 1:84 n.2.

55. Forster may have decided that "as *publishers*," Blackwood was not "a good firm," for although he "didn't mind much about money," Blackwood's terms for *Angels* were "really no money at all" (Lago and Furbank, *Letters*, 1:71); on the other hand, Forster may have been uneasy with Blackwood's very public Toryism, or his own company among the "chief Blackwood's writers," who in 1904 included, besides Joseph Conrad, "Zack," Sydney Grier, Mary Skrine, Beatrice Harraden, Storer Clouston, etc. F. D. Tredrey, *The House of Blackwood, 1804–1954* (Edinburgh: Blackwood, 1954), 193.

56. Oliver Stallybrass, Editor's Introduction, *Howards End*, Abinger ed. (London: Arnold, 1973), xii; Edward Arnold had been the reader for *Murray's Magazine* who had refused *Tess of the D'Urbervilles* in 1889 "virtually on the score of its improper explicitness." R. L. Purdy, *Thomas Hardy: A Bibliographical Study* (Oxford: Clarendon Press, 1968), 73.

57. Stallybrass, Editor's Introduction, *Howards End*, xiii.

58. B. J. Kirkpatrick, *A Bibliography of E. M. Forster*, 2d rev. imp. (London: R. Hart-Davies, 1968), 29; Derek Hudson, "Reading," in *Edwardian England*, ed. Nowell-Smith, 315.

59. P. N. Furbank, *E. M. Forster: A Life* (London: Secker and Warburg, 1977), 1:188–89.

60. Stallybrass, Editor's Introduction, *Howards End*, x; Stallybrass, Editor's Introduction, *A Room With a View*, xix; Wilfred Stone, " 'Overleaping Class': Forster's Problem in Connection," *Modern Language Quarterly* 39 (1978):386; Cyrus Hoy, "Forster's

Metaphysical Novel," *PMLA* 75 (1960):133; Furbank, *Forster,*
1:207; E. Barry McGurk, "Gentlefolk in Philistia: The Influence of
Matthew Arnold on E. M. Forster's *Howards End*," *English Literature
in Transition* 15 (1972):215.

61. Asa Briggs, "The Political Scene," 71; Kenneth D. Brown,
"The Anti-Socialist Union, 1908–49," in *Essays in Anti-Labour History,* ed., K. D. Brown (London: Macmillan, 1974), 236; Samuel
Hynes, *The Edwardian Turn of Mind* (Princeton: Princeton University Press, 1968), 172–211.

62. Lionel Trilling, *E. M. Forster* (London: Hogarth Press,
1951), 17; Peter Widdowson, *E. M. Forster's Howards End: Fiction as
History* (London: Sussex University Press, 1977), 26–28; Furbank,
Forster, 1:210.

63. E. M. Forster, *Howards End,* Abinger ed., ed. Oliver Stallybrass (London: Arnold, 1973), 266; all quotations are from this
edition and will be cited in the text.

64. Frederick L. Crews, *E. M. Forster: The Perils of Humanism*
(Princeton, N.J.: Princeton University Press, 1962), 34.

65. *B,* 96, n.s. (28 October 1910):52.

66. *The Author* 19, 9 (1 June 1909):241.

67. Oliver Stallybrass, ed., *The Manuscripts of Howards End,*
Abinger ed. (London: Arnold, 1973), 43; hereafter referred to as
"manuscript."

68. See Widdowson, *Forster's Howards End,* 12.

69. Ibid., 110.

70. John Ruskin, *The Stones of Venice* (vol. 2), in *The Works of John
Ruskin,* ed. E. T. Cook and A. Wedderburn (London: George
Allen, 1904), 10:37.

71. E. M. Forster, "The Challenge of Our Time," *Two Cheers for
Democracy,* Abinger ed., ed. Oliver Stallybrass (London: Arnold,
1972), 54.

72. John Sutherland, *Bestsellers* (London: Routledge and
Kegan Paul, 1981), 8; "the valorization of value takes place only
within this constantly renewed movement. The movement of
capital is therefore limitless." Karl Marx, *Capital,* trans. B. Fowkes
(Harmondsworth: Penguin, 1976), 1:253.

73. Sutherland, *Bestsellers,* 21.

74. Terry Eagleton, *Criticism and Ideology* (London: New Left
Books, 1976), 48.

Index

Act of 1842 (copyright), 59
Adam Bede (Eliot), 1, 46
Althusser, Louis, x, 102 n. 41
Altick, Richard, ix, 1, 40
Arnold, Edward, 77, 89, 93
Arnold, Matthew, 57–58, 62, 91–92
Associated Booksellers of Great Britain and Ireland, 81–83
Athenaeum, 14–15
Author, The, 44

Barnes, James J., 20
Beaty, Jerome, 51
Beethoven, Ludwig van, 95
Bell, Edward, 82
Bell, Moberly, 81
Bennett, Scott, 10–11
Bennett, Tony, 64–65, 68–69
Bentley, house of, 76, 80
Berne Convention, 79
Besant, Walter, 64
Bickers and Bush (bookseller), 19, 23, 24
Birrell, Augustine, 7
Blackwood, John, 36, 45–48, 56
Blackwood, William, 90, 118 n. 55
Blackwood's Magazine, 36, 47, 90
Bodichon, Barbara, 38
Bolton Weekly Journal, 63
Bookseller, The, 80, 85, 86
Booksellers: separation of publishers from, 4–6, 21–22; underselling by, 18–26, 80–83

Booksellers' Association, 18–20, 79
Booksellers' Question, 19–26, 28
Book War, 77, 81–83
Bourne, Fox, 60, 61, 64
Branded goods, 83–84, 86–88
Brief Summary in Plain Language of the Most Important Laws Concerning Women (Smith), 38
Brönte, Charlotte, 28
Brookfield, Jane, 28, 29, 34
Brookfield, William, 28, 29
Brown, Hablot K., 2
Brown, James M., 102 n. 44
Buckton, Bowdler, 85
Buried Life, The (Ray), 29
Butt, John, 1
Byron, Lord, 5

Cambridge University, 52, 54
Campbell, Lord, 19–20
"Candour in English Fiction" (Hardy), 74–75
Capitalism: book publishing transformation under, 3–4; and net books, 80, 89; and patriarchy, 38, 40–41; and professionalization, 41; and technology in publishing, 61. *See also* Commodity-text production
Carlyle, Thomas, 20, 67
Carter, John, ix, 26
Cassell's International Novels, 85
Chace Act, 79

Chapman, John, 19–21, 24, 35
Chapman and Hall, 1–3, 12–14
Churchill, Winston, 31
Circulating libraries, 23–27, 35,
37, 76–80, 83, 84. *See also*
Mudie's Library
Class journals, 64–65, 84–85
Clique journals, 64
Collins, Wilkie, 20
"Commerce of Literature, The"
(Chapman), 19
"Commercialization of Literature,
The" (Holt), 88
Commodity-text production, xi;
characteristics of, 7–10; and
Middlemarch, 49, 56; net books
as, 87–89, 98; petty-commodity
book production versus, 10–12,
20, 25, 27, 63, 79–80; *Pickwick
Papers* as, 12–17; *Tess* as, 69–75
Constable (publisher of *Edin-
burgh*), 5–6
Contagious Diseases Acts, 38
Copyright, 7–8, 57–60, 63, 79
Cornhill, The, 47–48
Corn Law, 20

Daily Mail, 91
Darwin, Charles, 20
Derbyshire Medical and Surgical
Society, 53
De Vries, Duane, 15
Dickens, Charles, 5, 6, 20, 31, 63,
88; *Pickwick Papers*, ix, xi, 1–3,
12–17, 63; *Sketches by Boz*, 1
Dicks v. Yates, 59
Discounts, trade, 25, 78, 80–82,
89–90
Donaldson case, 7
Don Quixote (Cervantes), 15–16
Duckworth and Company, 77

Eagleton, Terry, x, 15, 37, 40,
69–70, 100 n. 10
Early Life, The (Hardy), 75
Edinburgh, 5–6
Education Act of 1870, 79, 90
Eisenstein, Elizabeth, 101 n. 33

Eliot, George, 31, 36–56; *Adam
Bede*, 1, 46; *Middlemarch*, ix, xi,
36–38, 48–56; *The Mill on the
Floss*, 46–48; "Quarry for Mid-
dlemarch," 53; *Romola*, 47–48;
Silas Marner, 47
Encyclopaedia Britannica, 81
English Humourists, The (Thack-
eray), 31
*English Novel from Dickens to Law
rence, The* (Williams), 88–89
English Woman's Journal, 38, 45

Family Library, 10–11
Ford, George, 1, 2
Forster, E. M., 90–98; *Howards
End*, ix, 90–98; *The Longest
Journey*, 90; *A Room with a View*,
90, 91
Fortin, Nina, 40
Fortnightly Review, 57, 74
Furbank, P. N., 91

Gatrell, Simon, 73
Gettman, Royal, ix, 26, 76–77
Girton College, 38
Gladstone, William Ewart, 20–24,
35
Graphic, 63–64, 68–75
Griest, Guinevere, 26, 27, 76–77
Grundyism, 74–75

Harden, Edgar F., 29
Hardy, Barbara, 56
Hardy, Thomas, 64, 88; "Can-
dour in English Fiction," 74–
75; *The Early Life*, 75; *Tess of the
D'Urbervilles*, ix, 68–75
Heinemann, William, 85, 89, 90
Henry Esmond (Thackeray), ix, xi,
xii, 18–19, 25, 27–35
Hindess, Barry, 3
Hirst, Paul Q., 3
Hobsbawm, E. J., 3–4, 10
Holt, Henry, 88
Howards End (Forster), ix, 91–98
Howe, Ellic, 61
Hunt, Leigh, 20

Index

Index